For Paul ~
merry christmas!
xo ~
Ymda
2016

Olive or Twist?

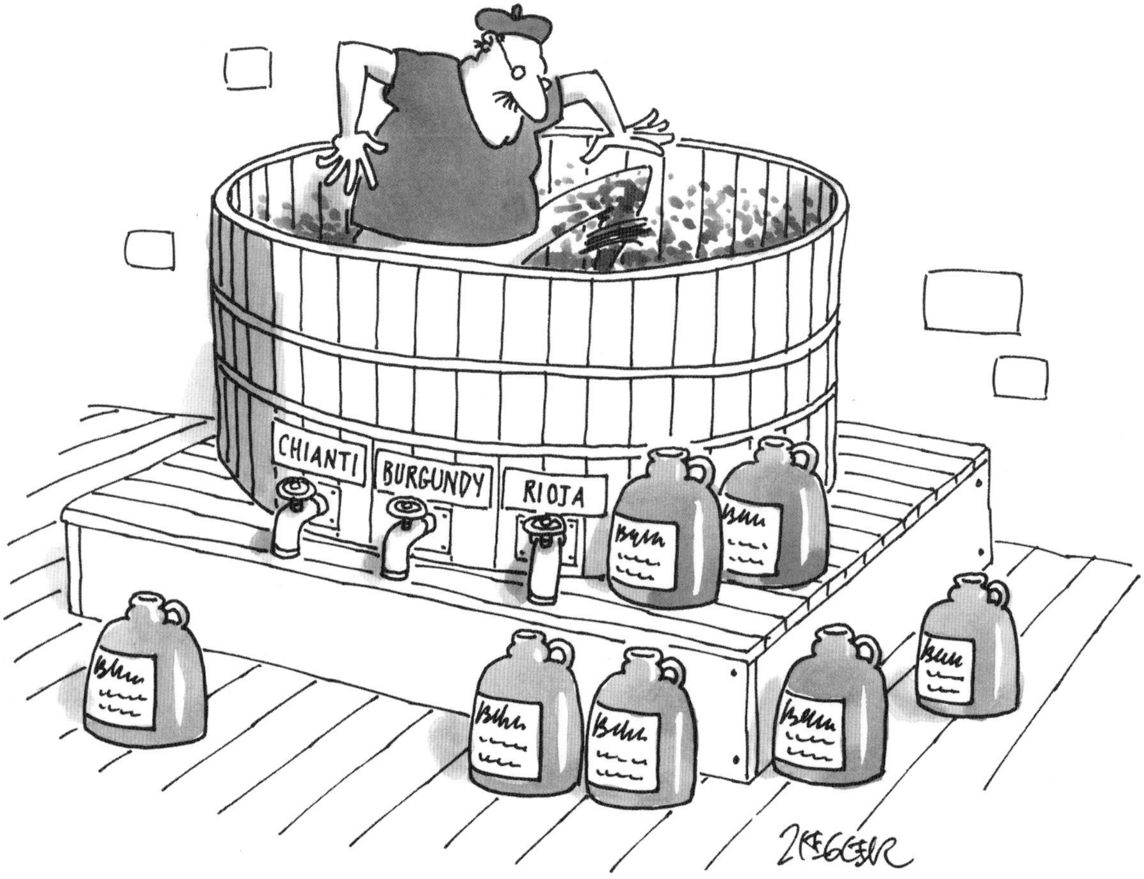
CHIANTI
BURGUNDY
RIOJA

Olive or Twist?

A Book of Drinking Cartoons

Jack Ziegler

Harry N. Abrams, Inc., Publishers

ACKNOWLEDGMENTS

Thanks to Christopher Sweet, Isa Loundon,
Sigi Nacson, Jane Cavolina, Steve Urban, Bill Wood,
Fred Ng, Uncle Tom, and The Glory Boys

Editor: Christopher Sweet
Editorial Assistant: Isa Loundon
Series Designer: Bob McKee
Production Manager: Norman Watkins

Library of Congress Cataloging-in-Publication Data

Ziegler, Jack.
  Olive or twist? : a book of drinking cartoons / by Jack
Ziegler.
    p. cm.
  Includes bibliographical references and index.
  ISBN 0–8109–5887–2 (hardcover : alk. paper)
  1. Drinking of alcoholic beverages—Caricatures and car-
toons. 2. American wit and humor, Pictorial. I. Title.

NC1429.Z47A4 2005
741.5'973—dc22
                          2004019496

The cartoons which appear on pages 8, 17, 122, and 124 are reproduced by special permission of *Playboy* magazine. Copyright © 2004 by *Playboy.*

Printed and bound in China

10 9 8 7 6 5 4 3 2 1

Harry N. Abrams, Inc.
100 Fifth Avenue
New York, N.Y. 10011
www.abramsbooks.com

Abrams is a subsidiary of

LA MARTINIÈRE
GROUPE

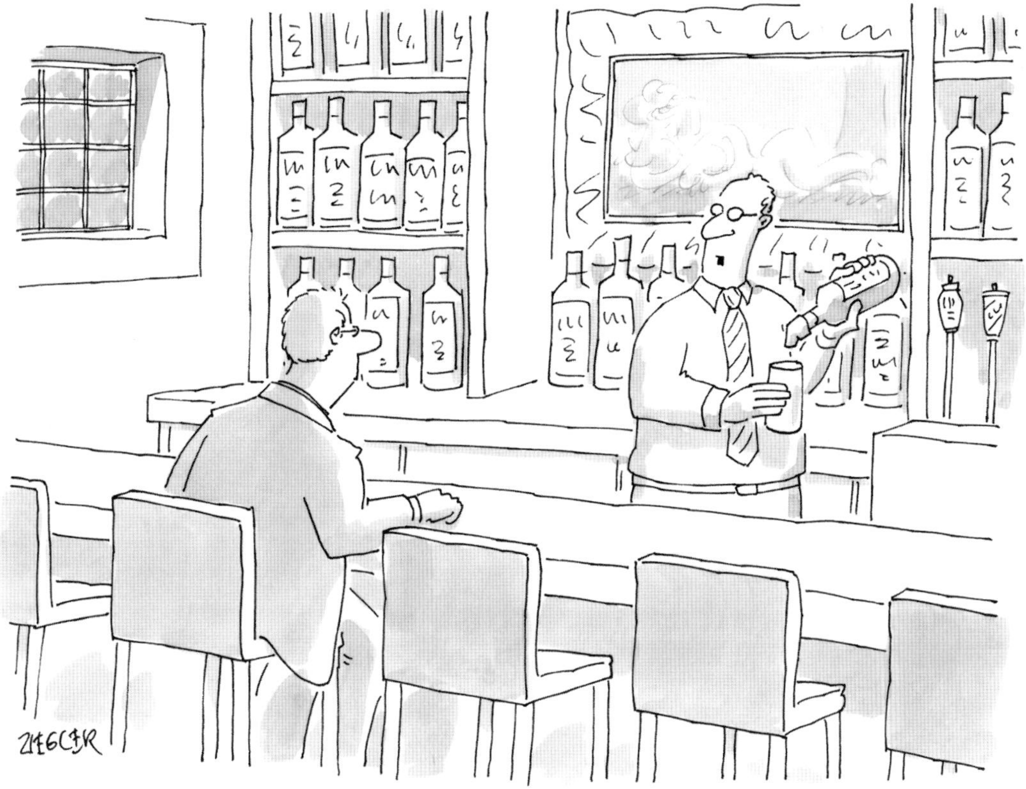
ZIEGLER

"Do you have a Frequent Drinkers card?"

To old friends: the people under the wharf in Monterey

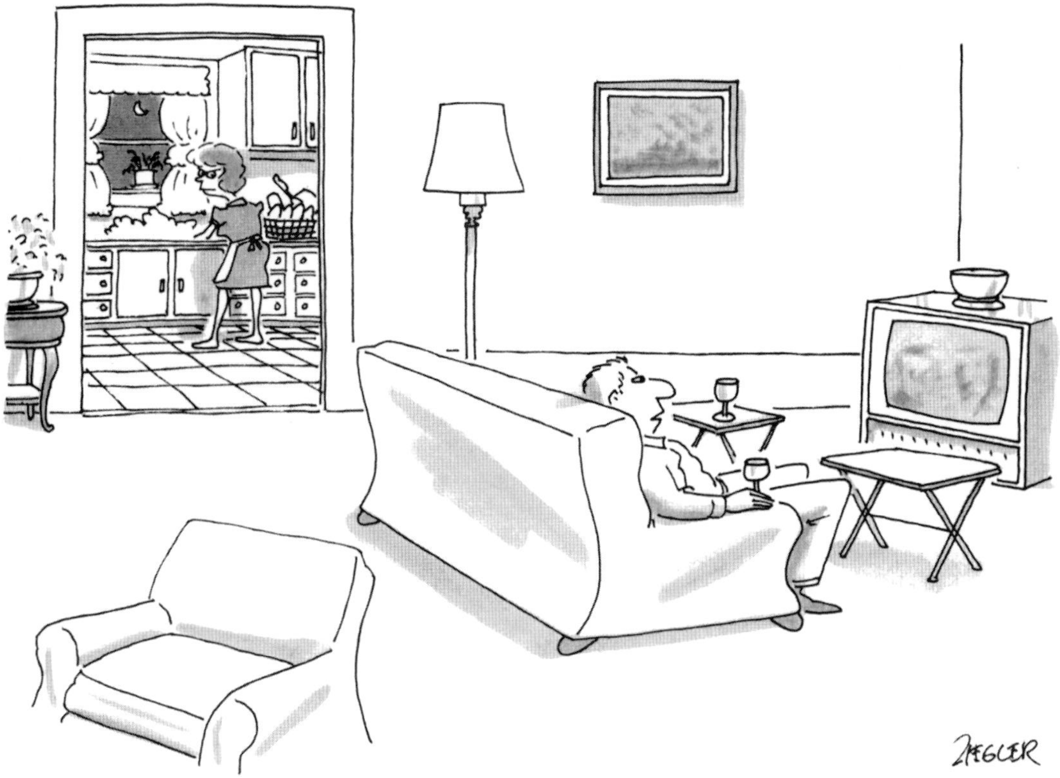
ZIEGLER

"By the way, hon, great food, great wine, great you."

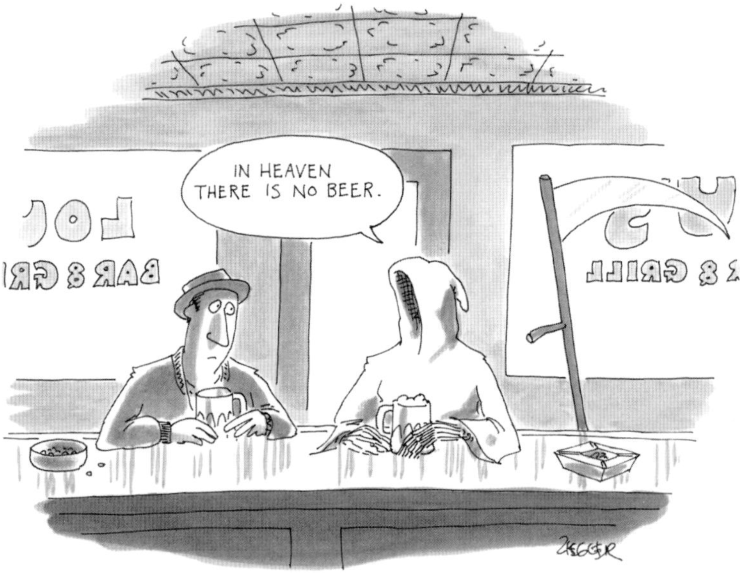
IN HEAVEN
THERE IS NO BEER.

Introduction

In the early Sixties, I needed some extra cash to pay for the subway tokens that would get me from my parents' house in Queens to the college I was attending up in the Bronx, not to mention some money for the occasional sandwich at the Student Center, a Saturday night date, or a new pair of chinos to go with the required jacket and tie.

Fortunately the school had a Placement Office and on their bulletin board one day I spotted a potential job that looked to be right up my alley—Guest Relations at CBS-TV, just down the subway line in Manhattan. After a breezy interview with a rather eccentric young executive, one of whose duties was overseeing and scheduling the gentlemen of Guest Relations, I was hired. We were called pages, and our job, essentially, was to act as ushers for the live and taped shows that CBS was producing at Studio 50, on Broadway, and Studio 52, located around the corner on West 54th Street.

"Wow," I rejoiced. "Showbiz at last!"

The pages' locker room was in the basement beneath 50, and labyrinthine underground passageways connected the two studios. I eventually found my way in these confusing, darkened corridors, however, and was soon standing under the bright lights of such shows as "Ed Sullivan," "Garry Moore," "Jackie Gleason," "College Bowl," "I've Got a Secret," "What's My Line?," and "Ted Mack's Original Amateur Hour," to name a few.

The job required guiding the audiences in and out with a minimum of hassle and keeping them in their seats. No flash bulbs, no moving around or other excessive behavior during tape- or air-time. Crowd control, in other words. Once, during a Sullivan show, one attendee down front was reacting inappropriately and hugely to some comedian on stage and, after the closing credits had rolled, Ed called this person up on stage and excoriated her roundly for disrupting the show and possibly throwing off the performer's timing. Humiliated, she left the theater in tears. Ordinarily it would have been the page's job to discreetly shush this person during the next commercial, but, alas, it was the end of the show and no more words from Ajax or Salem Cigarettes or whatever were to be had.

That's right. I said Salem, for these were the carefree days when cigarettes were still allowed to be advertised (and smoked) on network TV. In fact, as audiences were filing into some quiz shows, the pages would hand out free little four-cigarette packets—thoughtfully provided by the kind folks at Marlboro or Kool or Salem—to our attendees, whether they were smokers or not. These four-packs were supplied to us in regular-sized cigarette cartons and any leftovers were generously provided gratis to the pages, whether we were smokers or not.

It was here, at the tender age of nineteen, that I became an inveterate smoker for the next seventeen years. After all, who was I to look a gift horse in the mouth? I was an impoverished student, and to cast aside any free handout would have been insane. And so, for my first three years as a butthead, I smoked at the expense of Big Tobacco. Man, oh man, I mused, the laugh sure was on them.

When work was done, some of the pages, stagehands, seamstresses, June Taylor Dancers, and other Runyonesque types would retire to a fine little boîte a few doors uptown from Studio 50 called the China Song. Here, Freddy Ng, the proprietor, and Uncle Tom, the bartender, would provide us with all the pork fried rice and booze we could afford. At the China Song, we all became garrulous, witty, and intelligent beyond our wildest dreams. Nightly, we decided the fate of the universe as we smoked our complimentary cigarettes and laughed in the face of neglected homework or lack of sleep because, deep down, we knew that both could be accomplished the following morning on the train back up to the Bronx.

I can still name and clearly picture—and occasionally celebrate in cartoons—most of the people who hung out at the Song after the studio lights had been dimmed. Among the pages were not only students, but out-of-work actors, struggling writers, future restauranteurs, inveterate con men, and a performing chimp or two. It was back in a time when the worst we had to worry about was the Cold War which, being slightly intoxicated kids, we pretty much ignored; and that maybe explains, or doesn't explain, why one night Bill Wood, from the Wardrobe Department, took one look at the double scotch Uncle Tom had just passed to him and thrust his hand deep into the glass, coming up with a fistful of ice, which he then flung across the room.

"What's with all the goddamn ice, Tom?" he sneered. "Who the hell do you think I am? Sonja Henie??" he shouted. "I came here to drink," he shrieked, "not skate!!!"

It was another night at the China Song and things were just starting to warm up.

—*Jack Ziegler, Las Vegas, 2004*

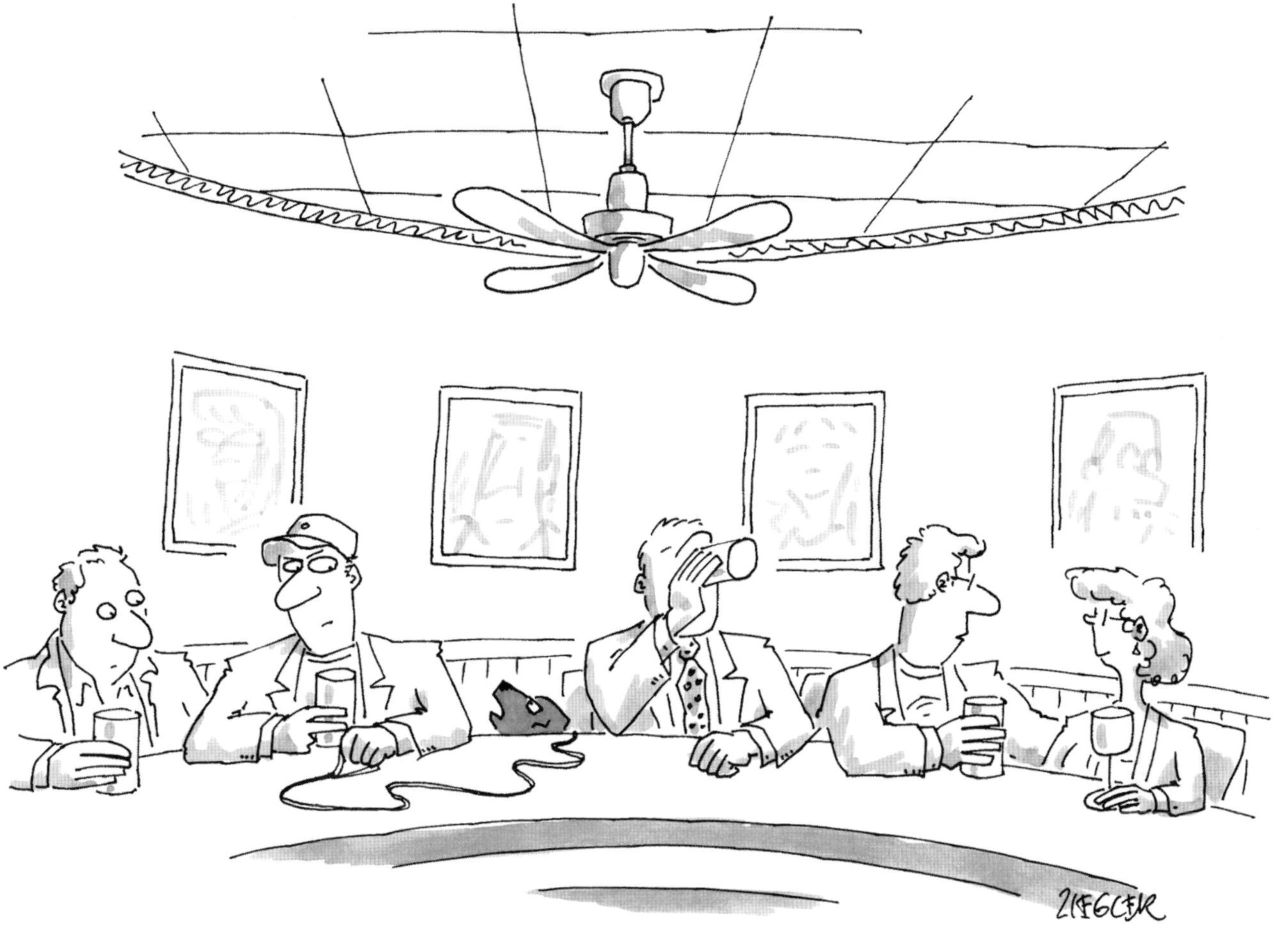

"Hey! You call this a walk?"

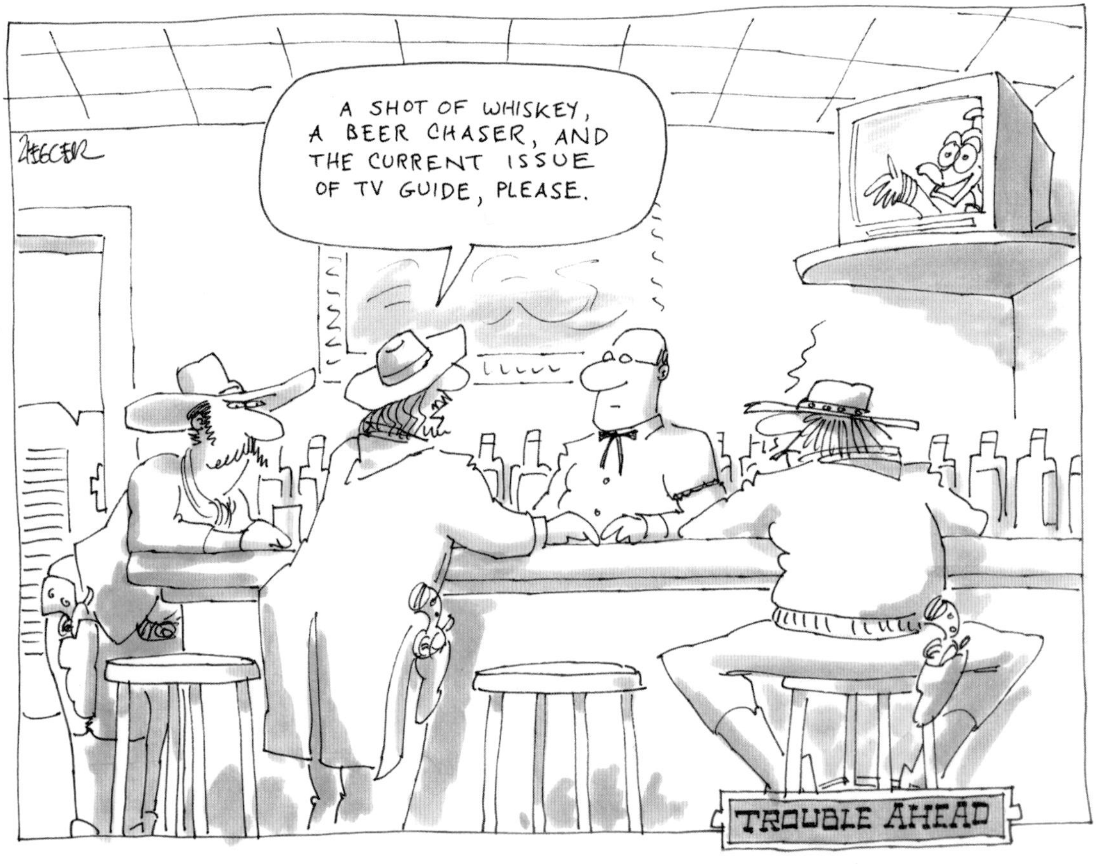
ZIEGLER
A SHOT OF WHISKEY, A BEER CHASER, AND THE CURRENT ISSUE OF TV GUIDE, PLEASE.
TROUBLE AHEAD

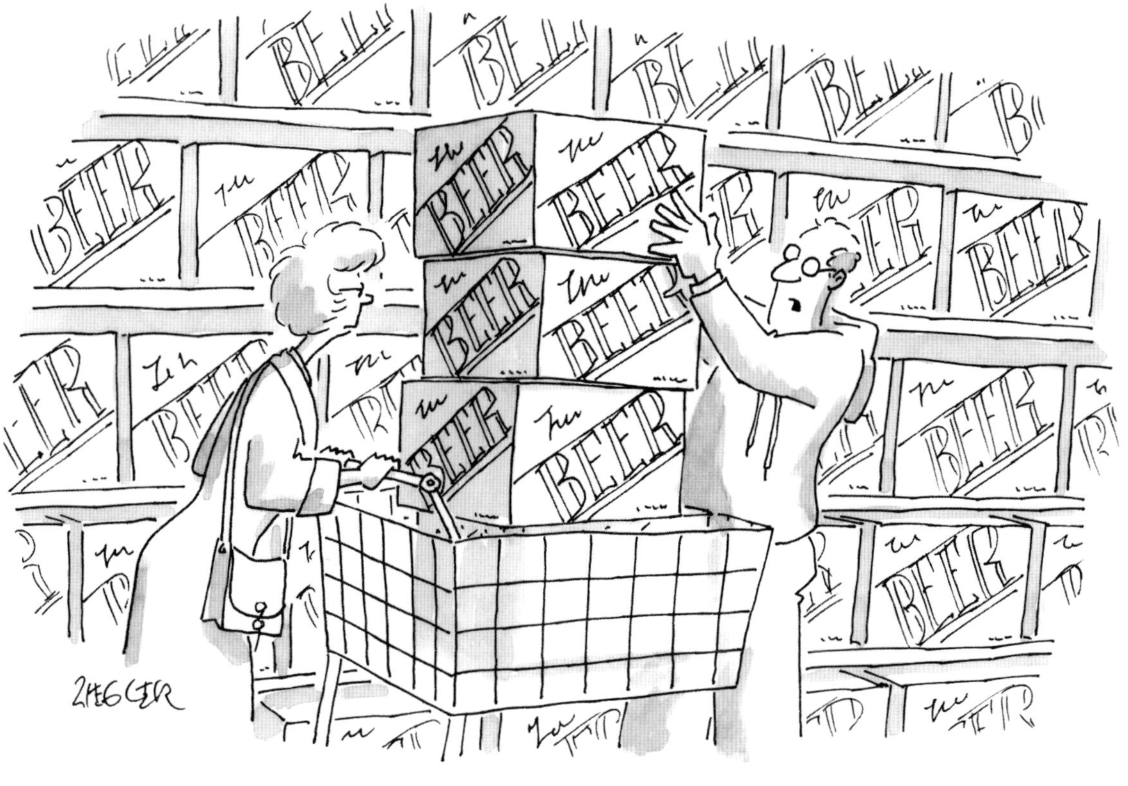
BEER
ZIEGLER

"O.K. That's my list. You got anything on your list?"

My First Mistake
ZIEGLER
orange juice
coffee
coffee
water
water
water
ginger ale
beer
beer
beer
beer
beer
scotch
scotch
wine
wine
wine
Brandy
sleep (my first mistake)
orange juice

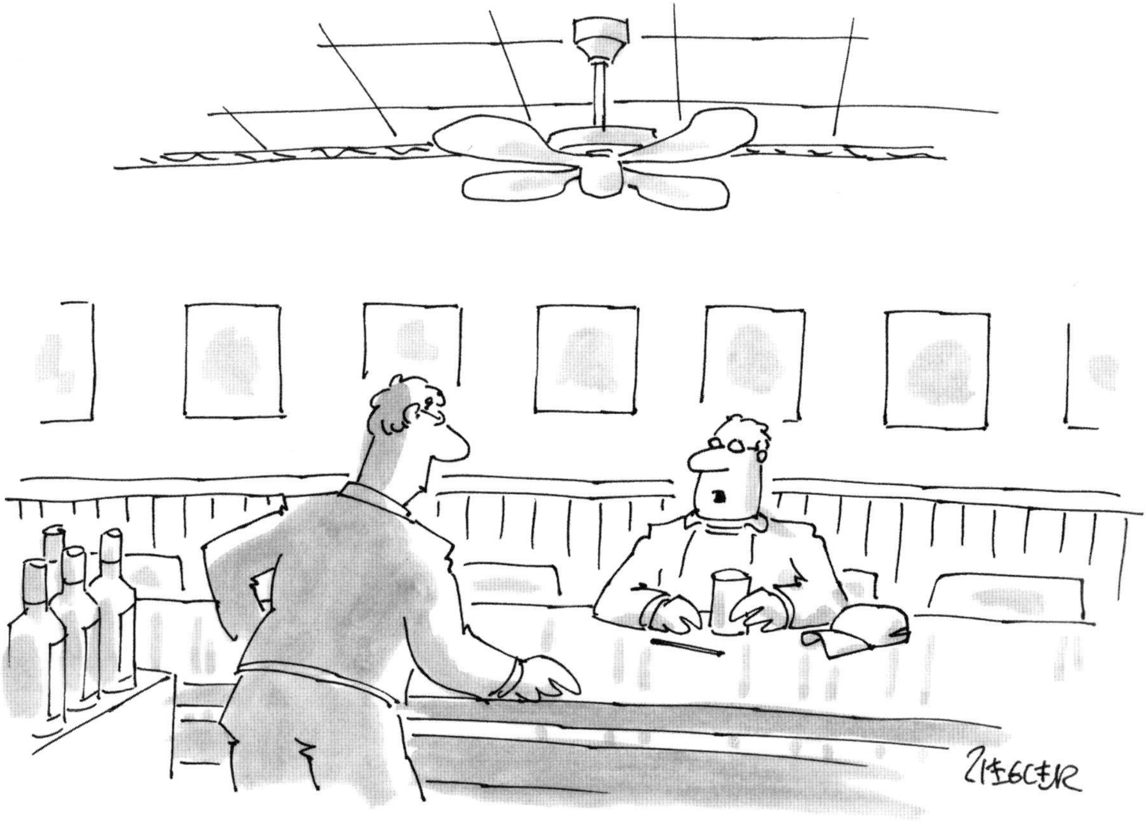
ZIEGLER

"They tell me I'm highly respected in my field, should I choose to pursue it."

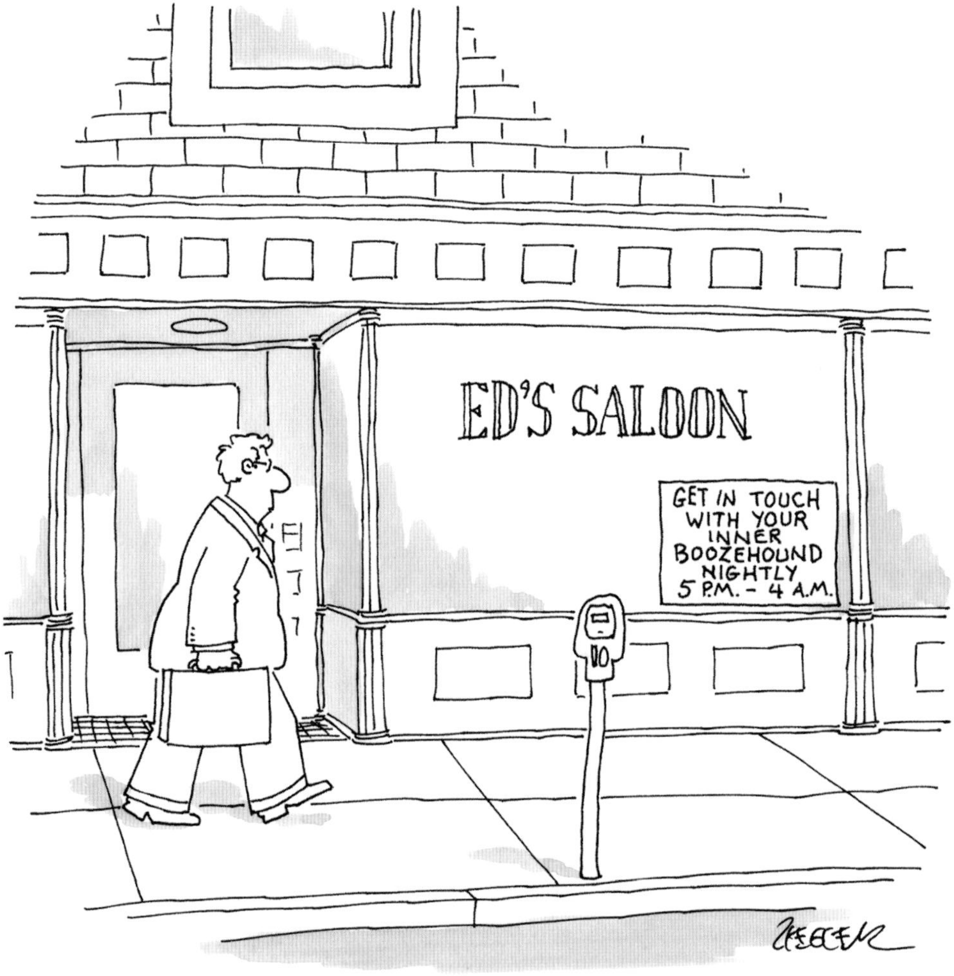

ED'S SALOON
GET IN TOUCH WITH YOUR INNER BOOZEHOUND NIGHTLY 5 P.M. - 4 A.M.

"I don't know if I've mentioned this before, Greg, but you are a very attractive man."

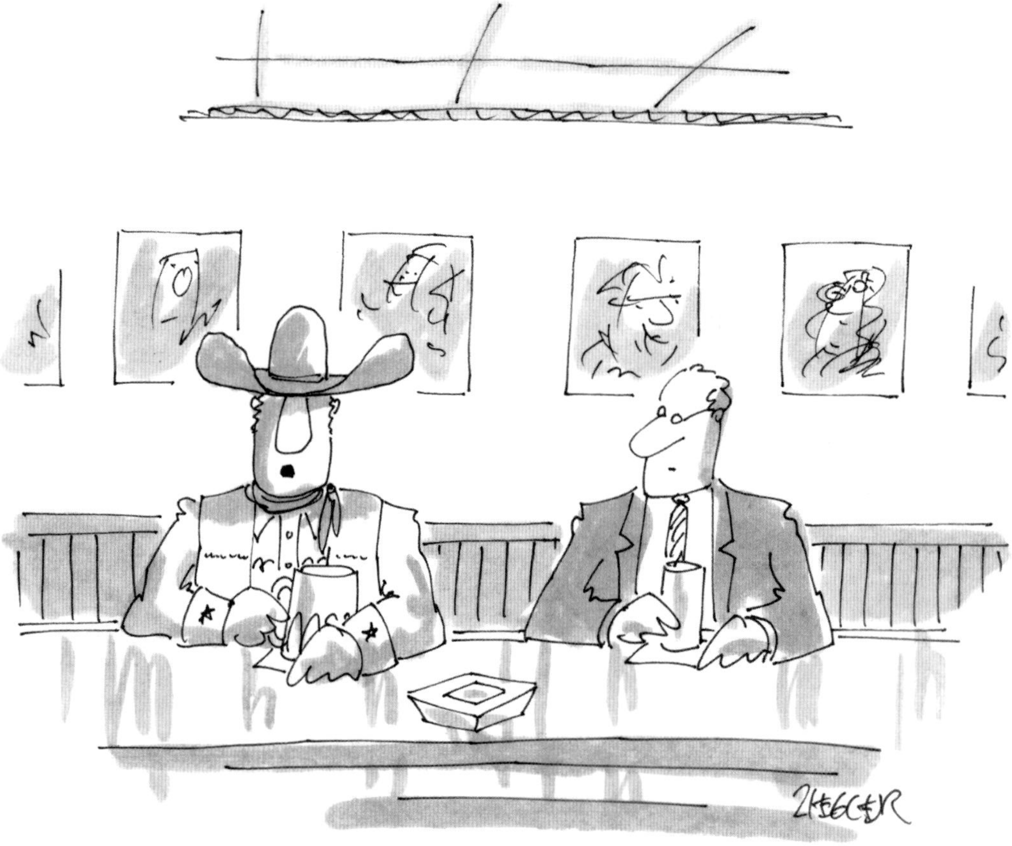
ZIEGLER

"These boots were made for drinking."

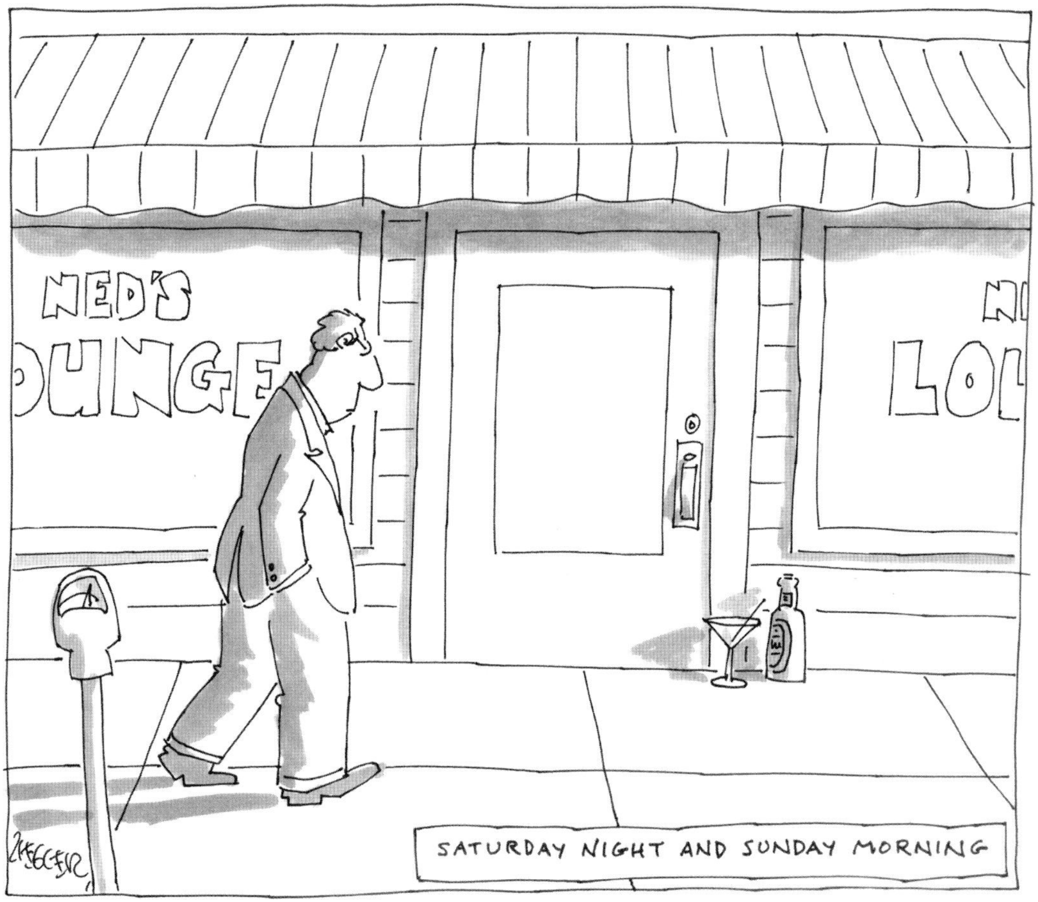
NED'S

SATURDAY NIGHT AND SUNDAY MORNING

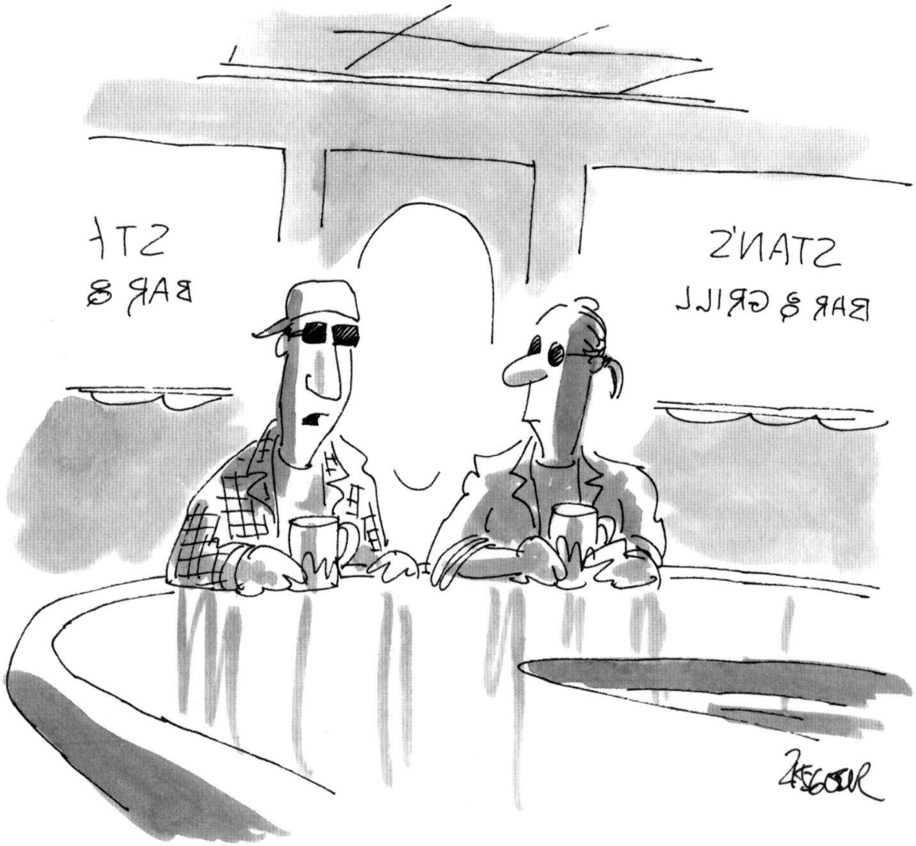
STAN'S
BAR & GRILL

"We seem to be split along party lines. I want to pretty much party for the rest of eternity and she doesn't."

"*Miss Coleman, would you step in here, please, and take a martini.*"

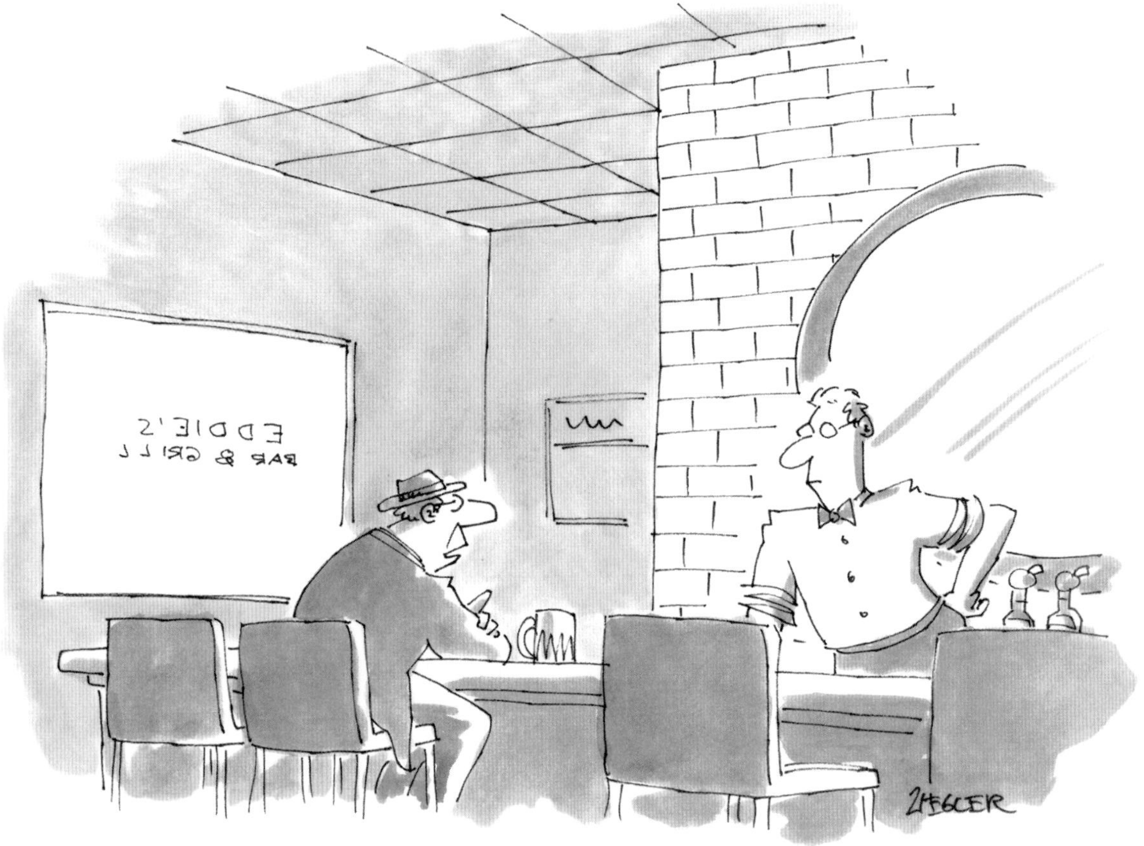
EDDIE'S
BAR & GRILL
ZIEGLER

"Promise me, Eddie, that when I pass away, you won't make the announcement until after the closing bell so as not to affect the stock market."

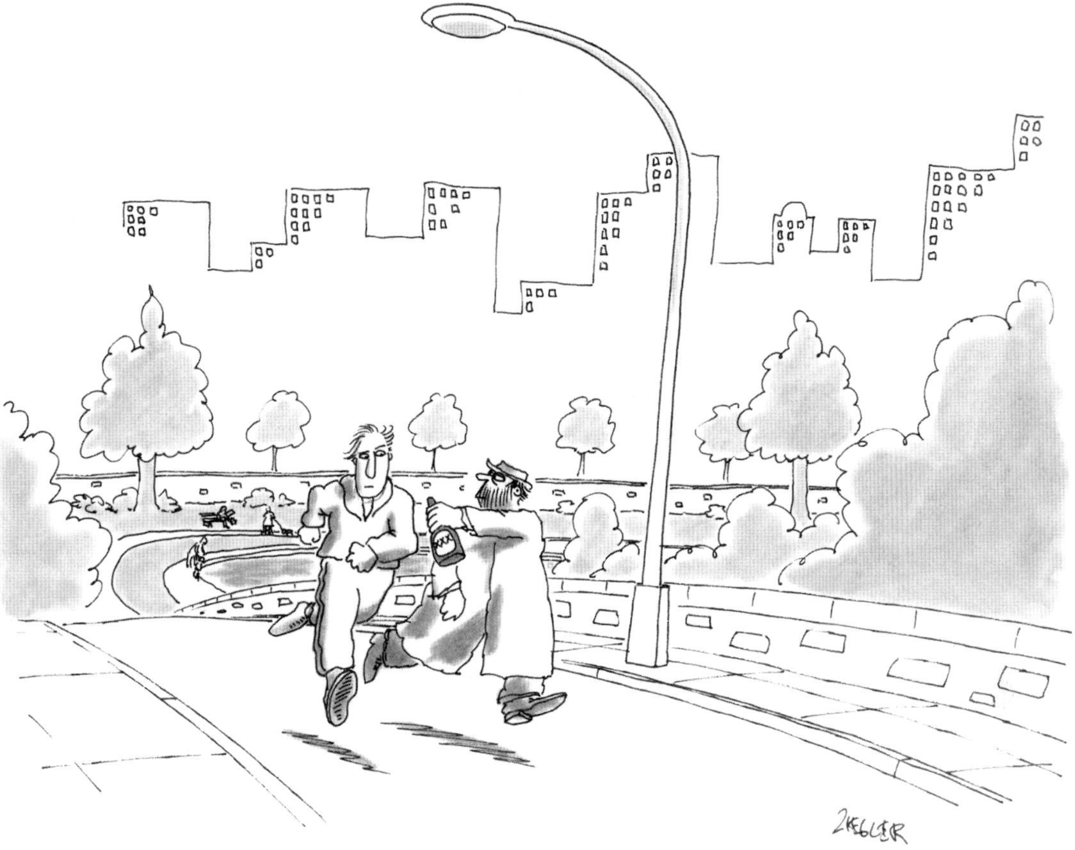
ZIEGLER

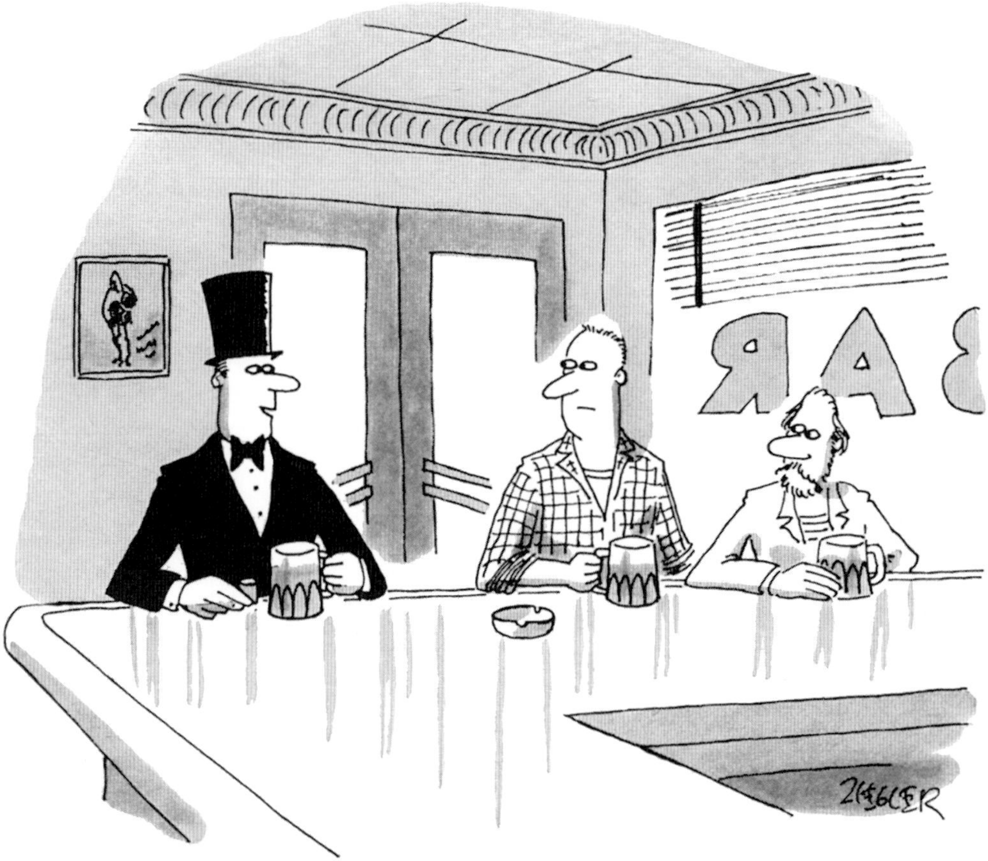
ZIEGLER

"I get no kick from champagne."

TRULY AFFORDABLE BEAUJOLAIS
1998
ED'S VINTNERS BRONX, N.Y.
ZIEGLER

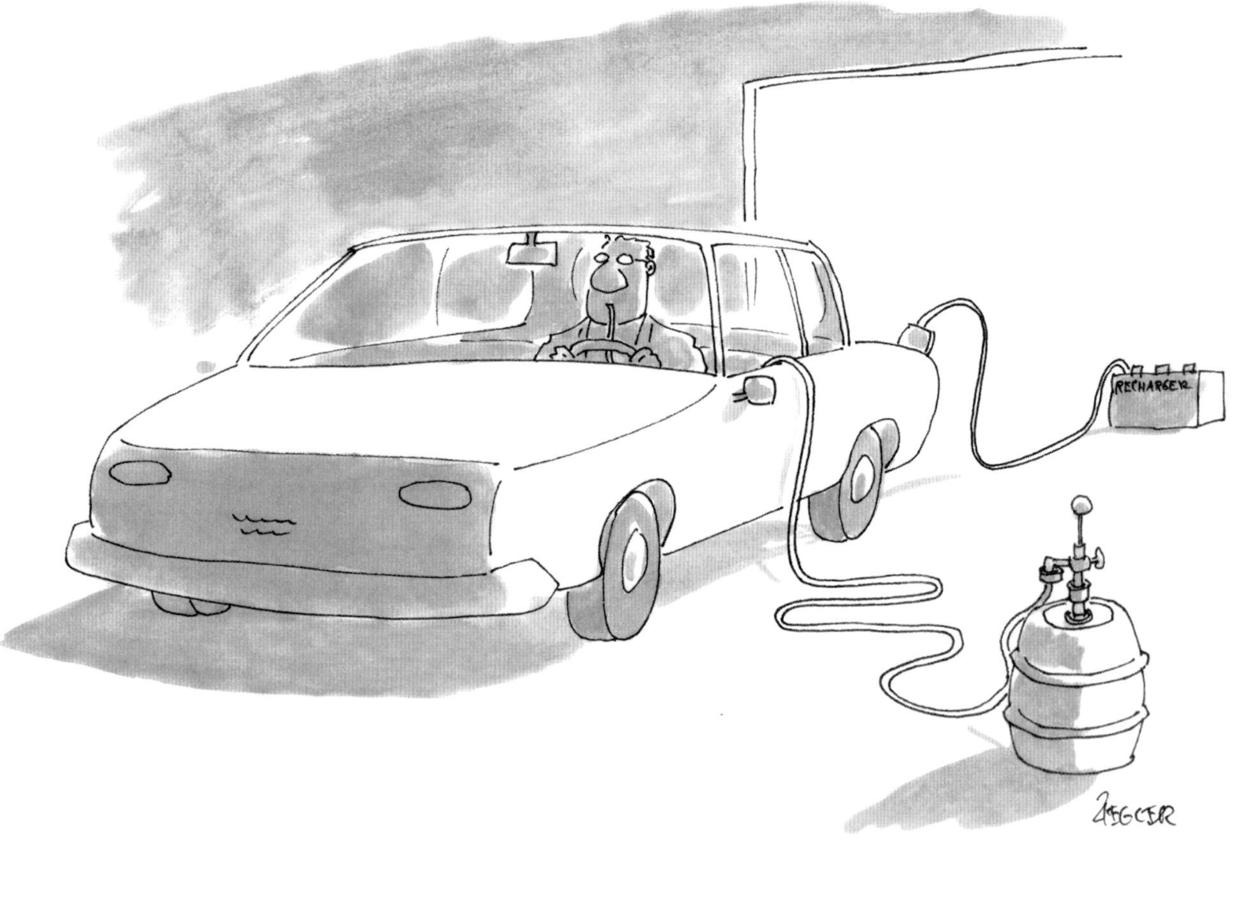
RECHARGER
ZIEGLER

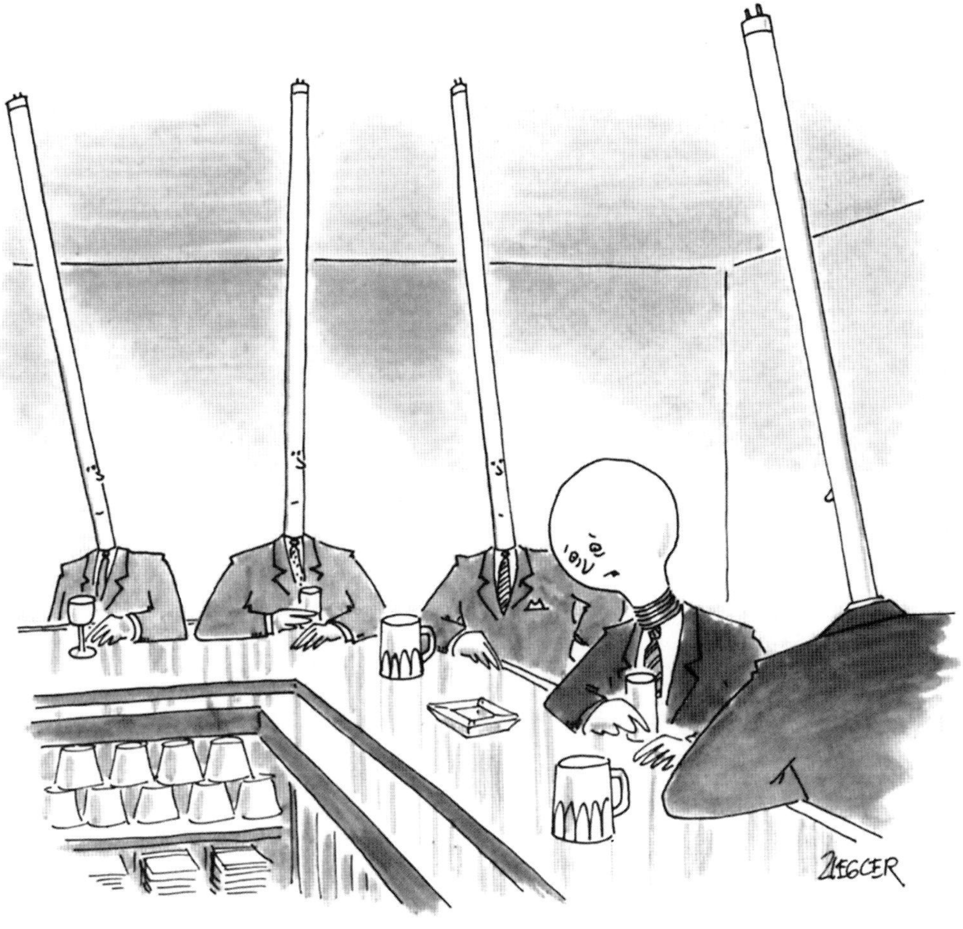
ZIEGLER

"Laugh if you will, but my kind once ruled the earth."

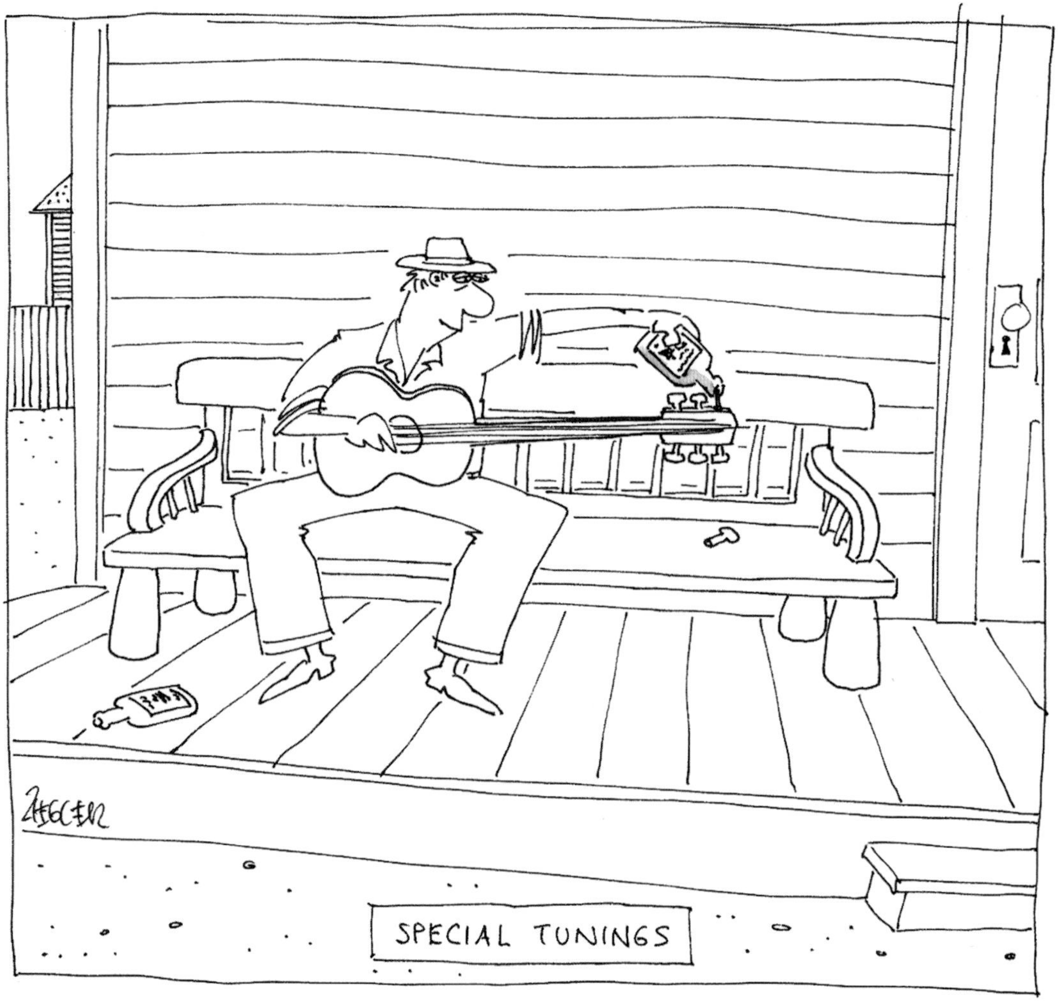
ZIEGLER
SPECIAL TUNINGS

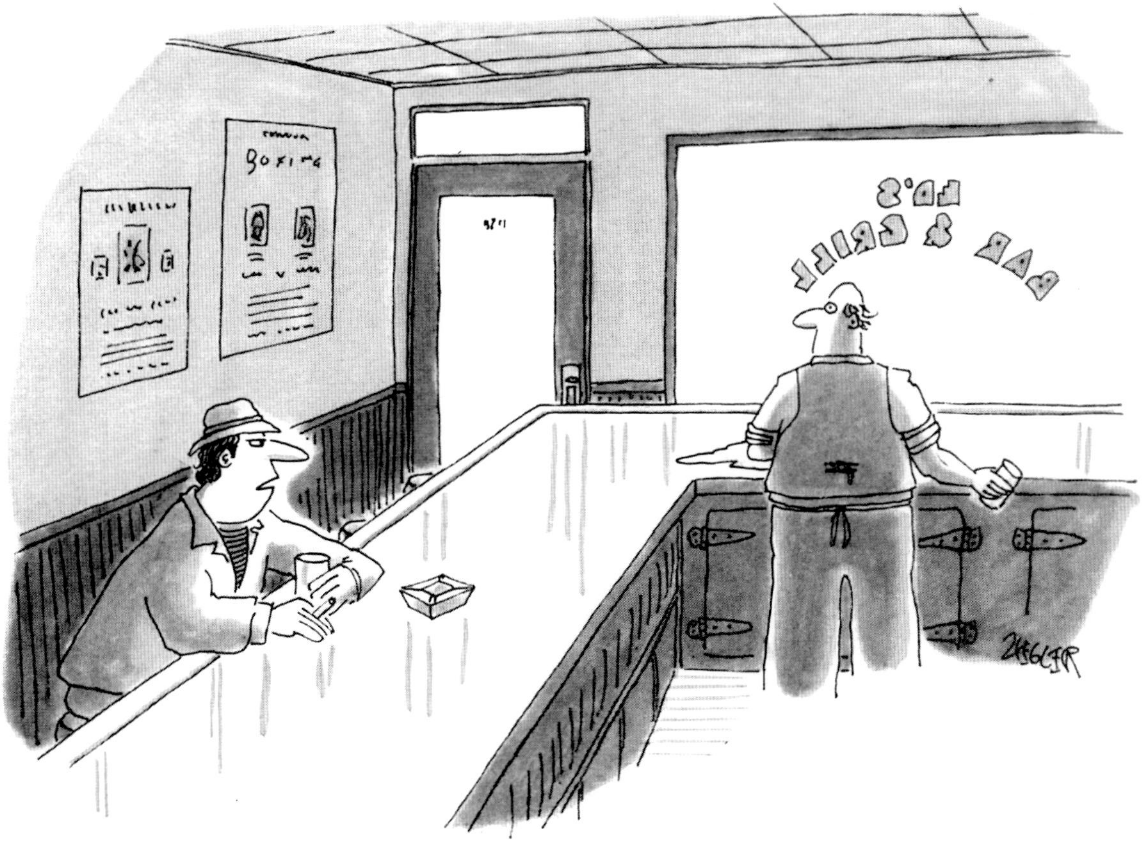
BOXING
ED'S
BAR & GRILL
ZIEGLER

"It was the best of times, it was the worst of times—Hey! I'm talking to you! It was the best of times . . ."

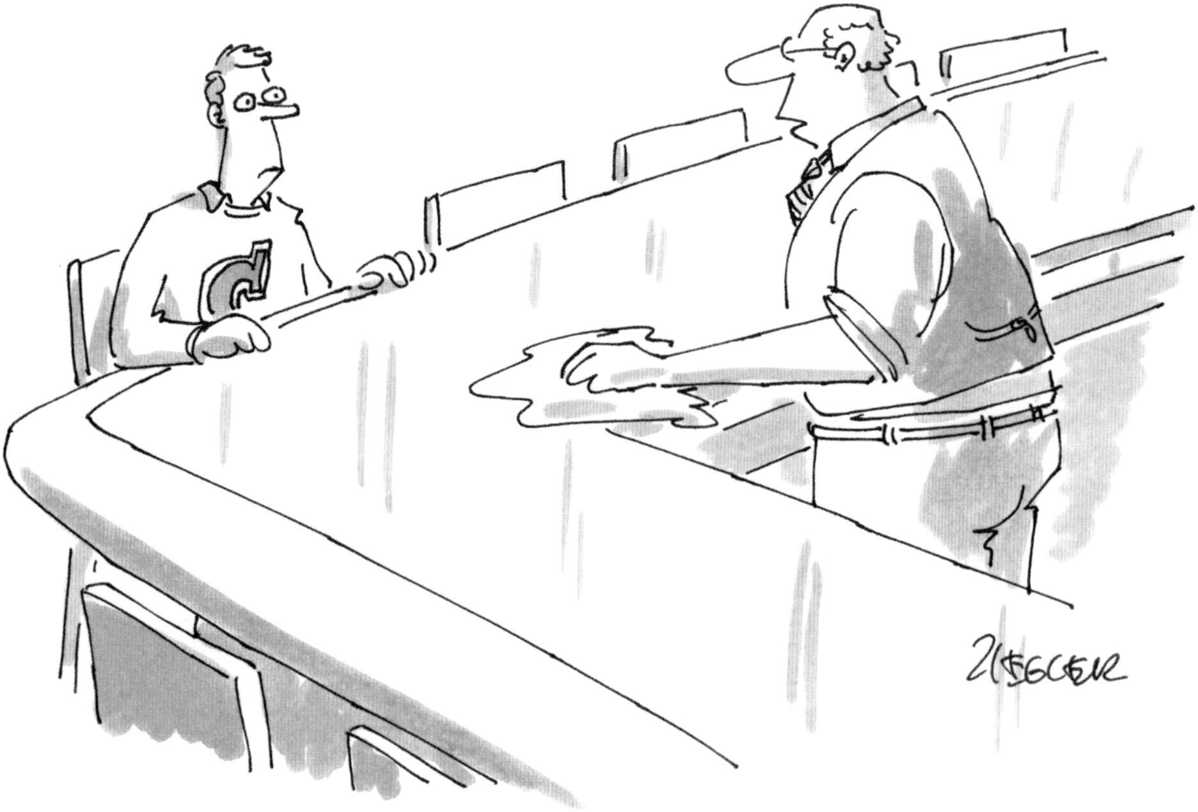
ZIEGLER

"Sorry, kid. No off-campus drinking until you're twenty-one."

"*I was once in dire straits, much as you are, my friend, and then I discovered the '97 Napa Valley cabernets.*"

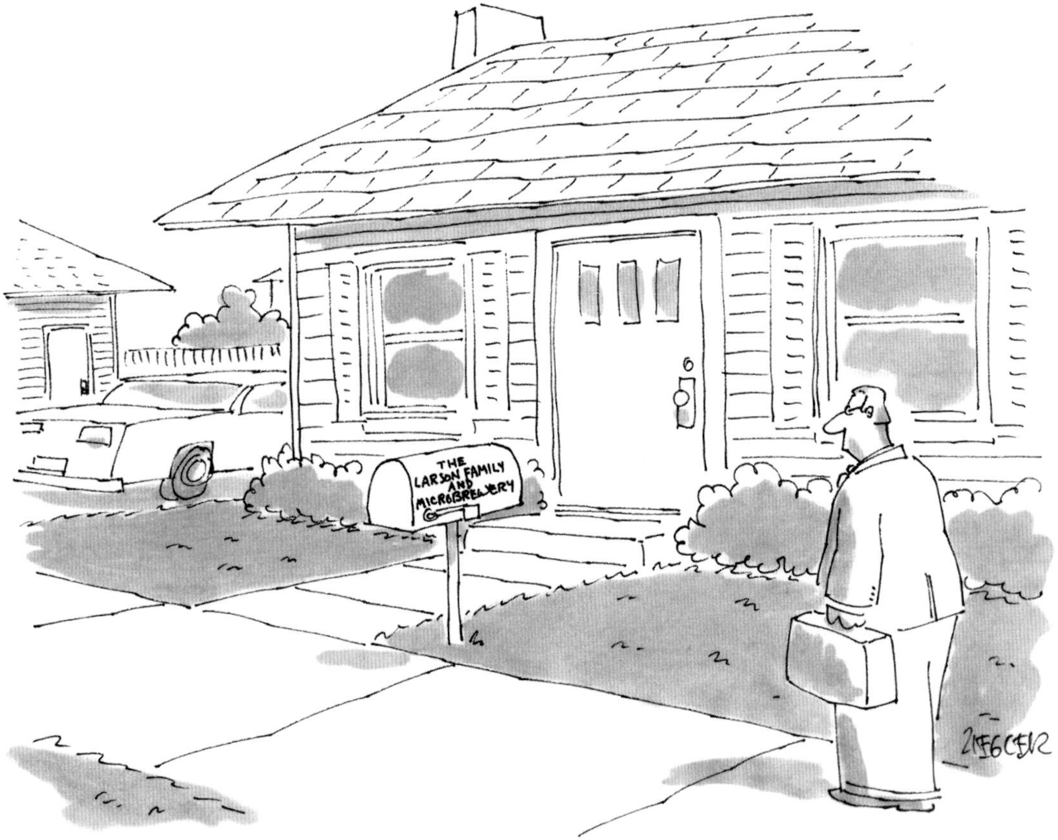
THE
LARSON FAMILY
AND
MICROBREWERY

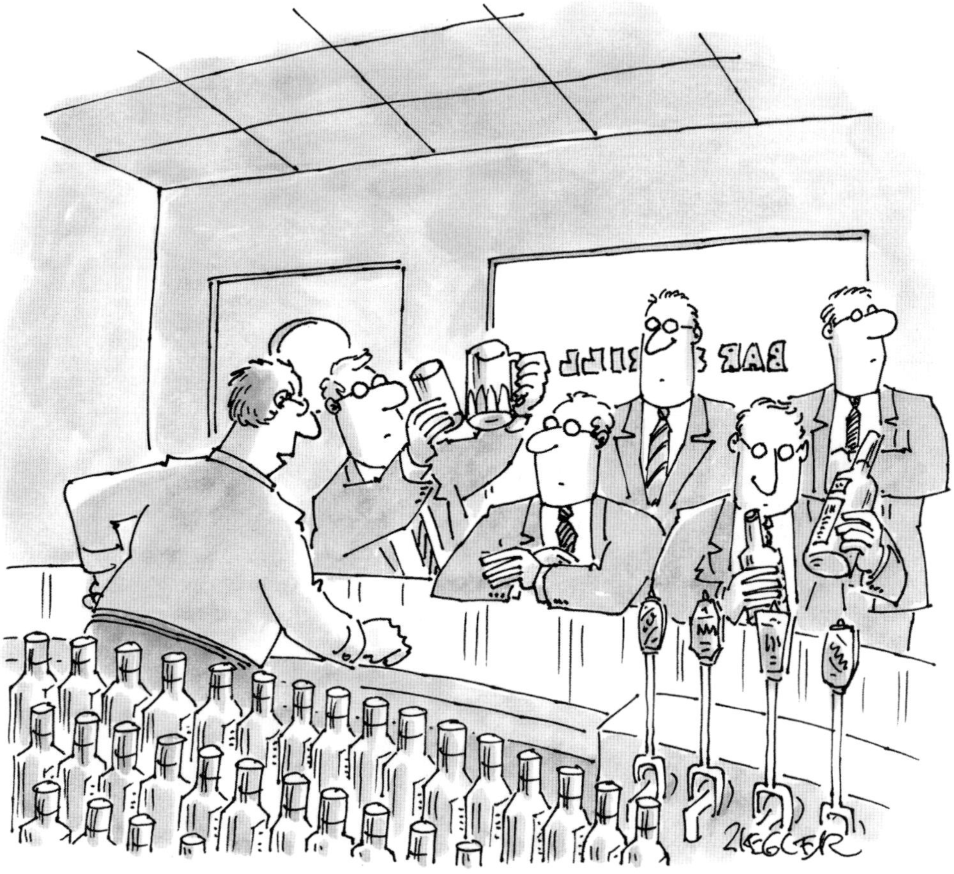
ZIEGLER

"I hardly think a transition team is necessary, Ed, in order to switch from beer to Scotch."

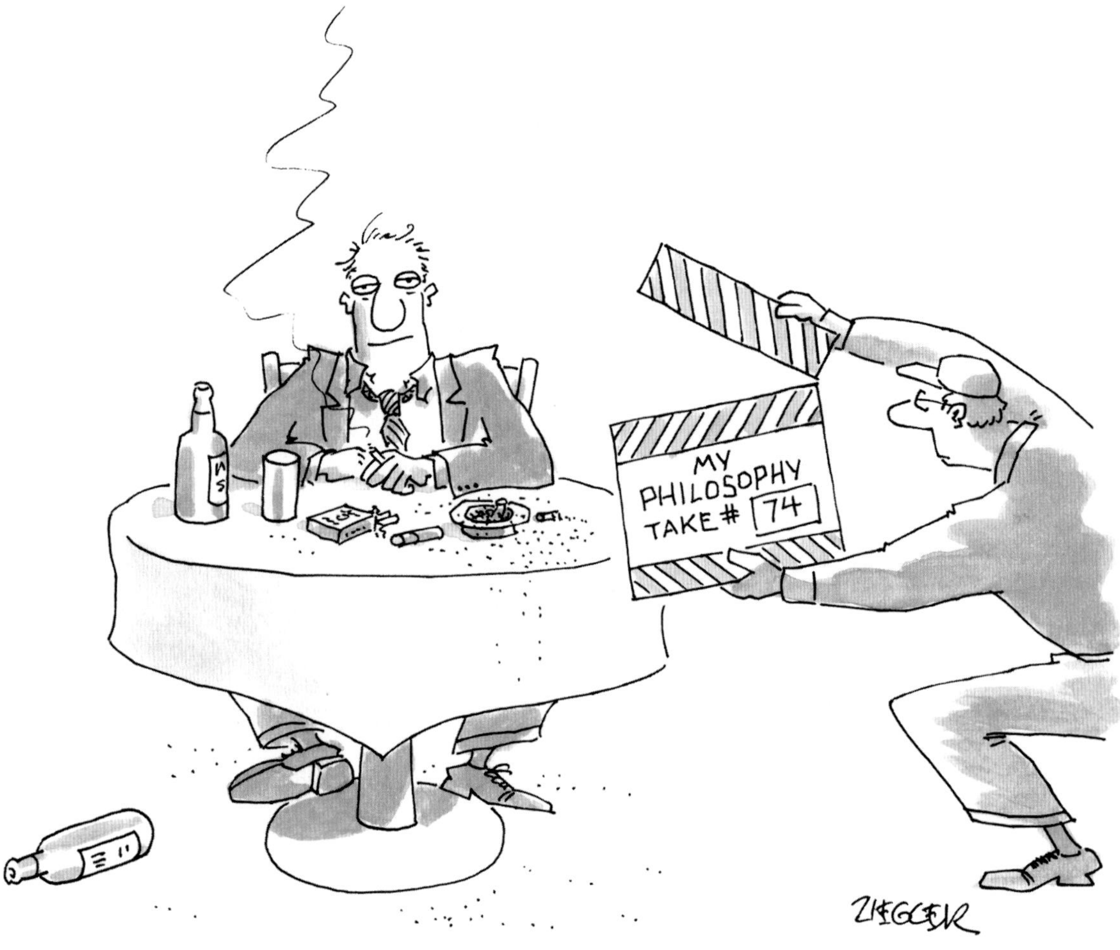
MY
PHILOSOPHY
TAKE # 74
ZIEGLER

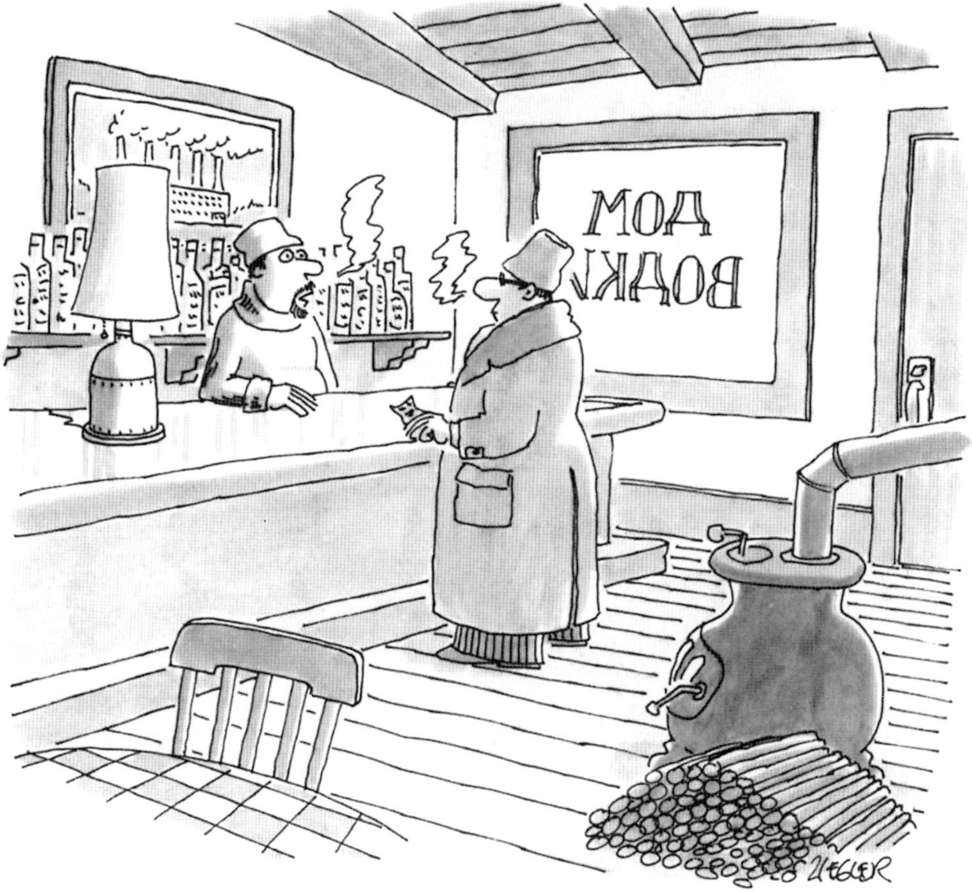
ZIEGLER

"In addition to our house vodka, we carry these distinctive imports: Gilbey's, Gordon's, Wolfschmidt, and Fleischmann's."

"*What with these endless hangovers, I'm beginning to miss the good old days of heroin chic.*"

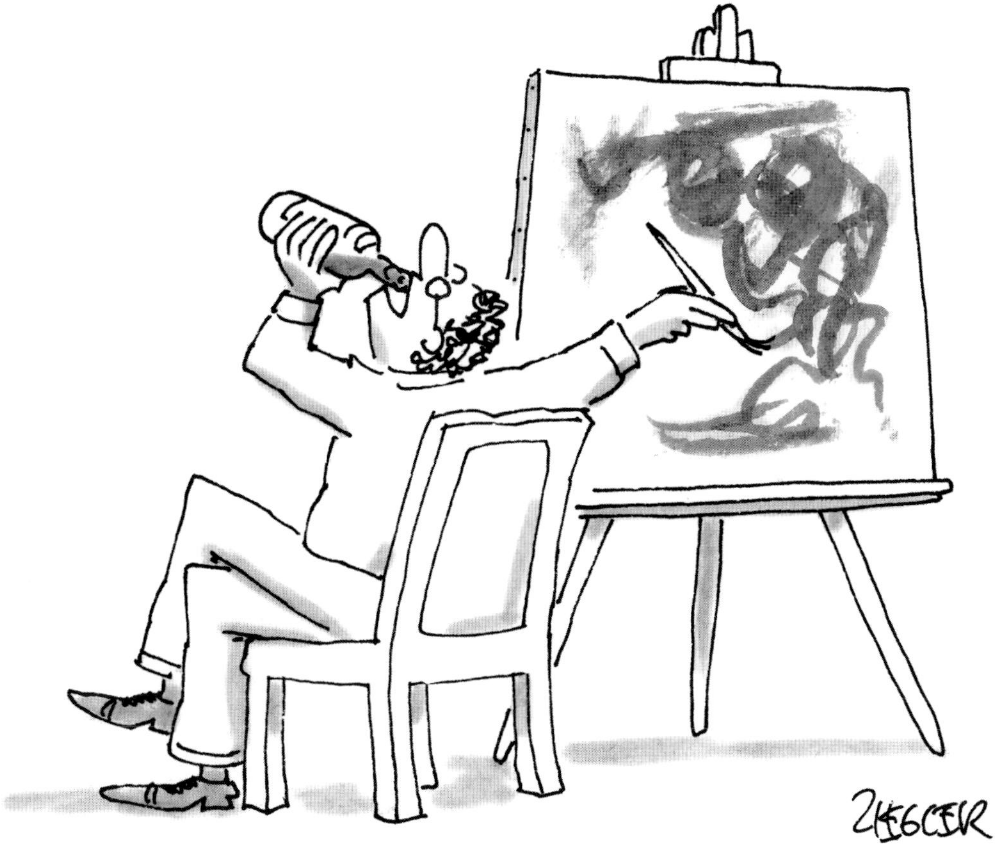
ZIEGLER

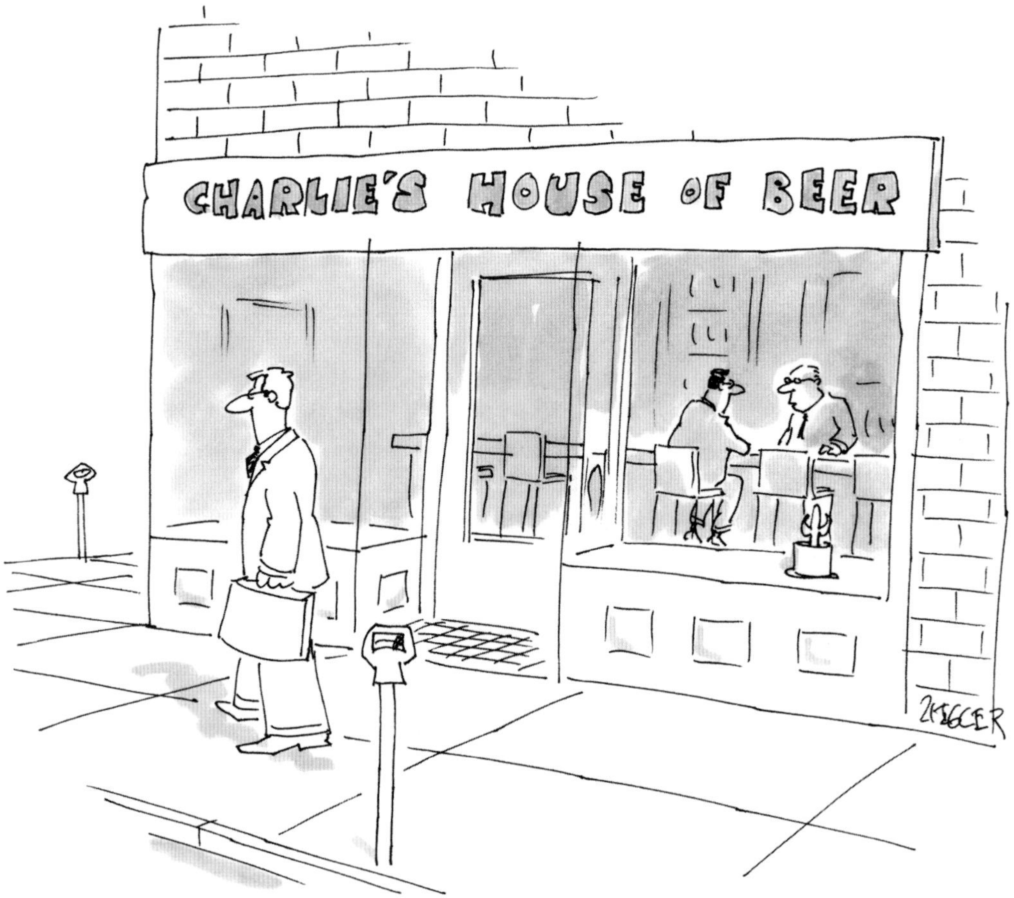
CHARLIE'S HOUSE OF BEER

"Import, Domestic, Micro, or Crap?"

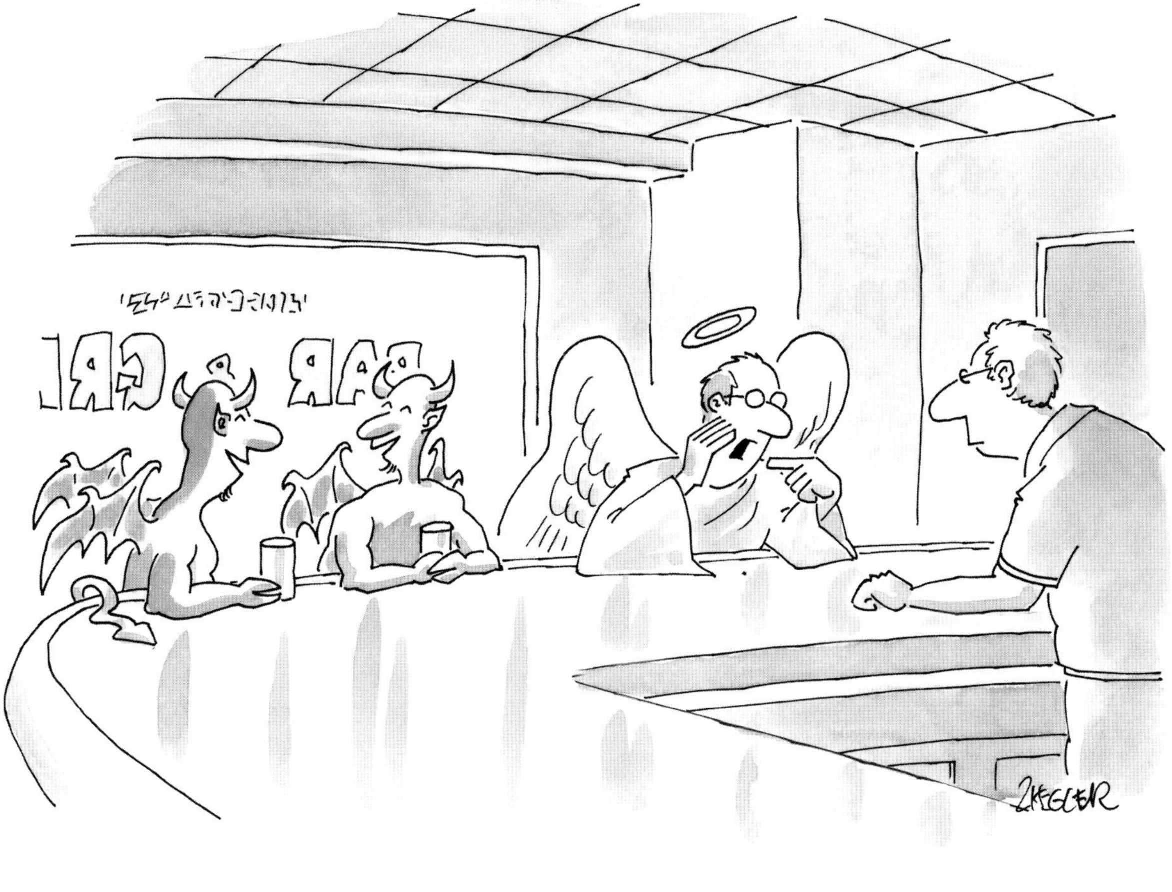
ZIEGLER

"I'll have whatever they're having."

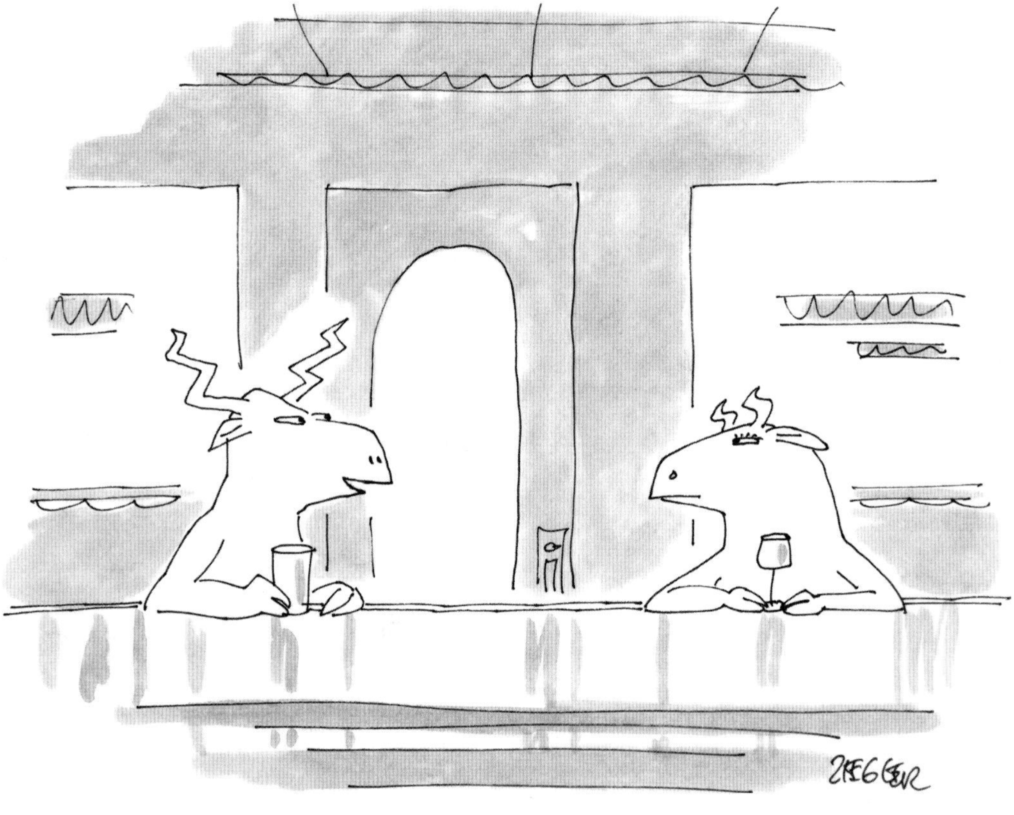
ZIEGLER

"Excuse me, Miss, but are you by any chance in estrus?"

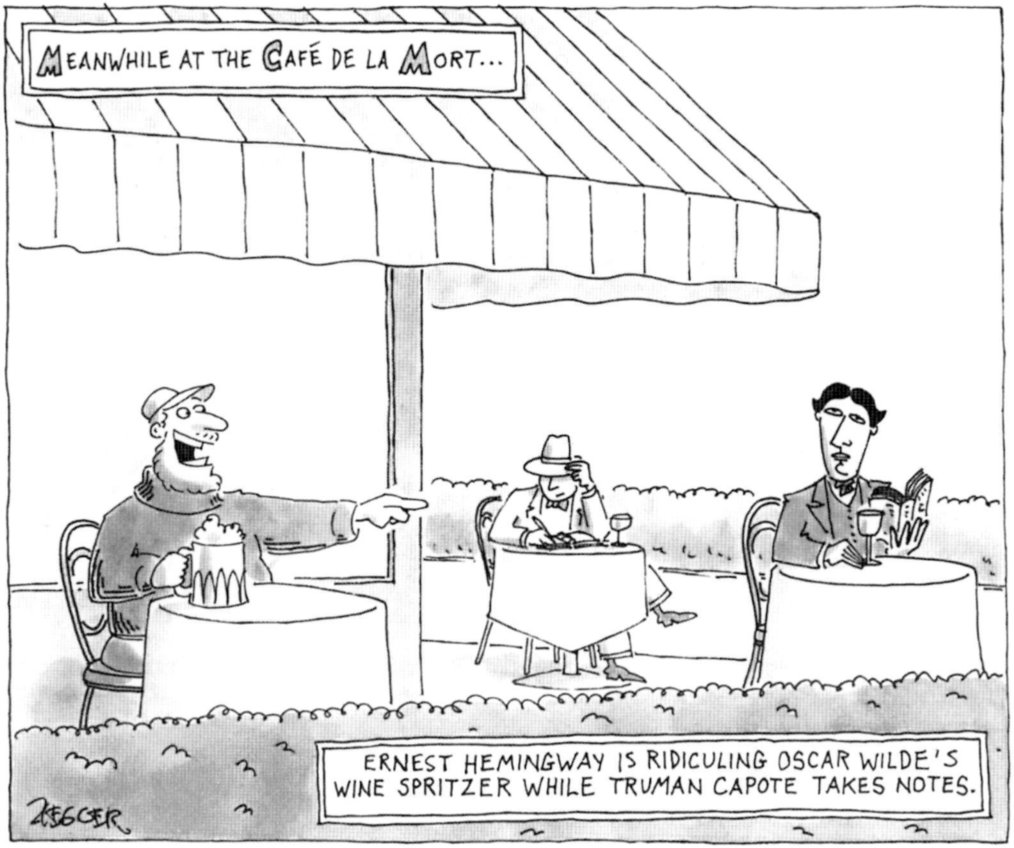
MEANWHILE AT THE CAFÉ DE LA MORT...
ERNEST HEMINGWAY IS RIDICULING OSCAR WILDE'S WINE SPRITZER WHILE TRUMAN CAPOTE TAKES NOTES.
ZIEGLER

"*Here's to our love, baby, unless, of course, death, another chick, or a move to the coast do us part.*"

"I may not be in for a while, Eddie. My wife and I have decided to normalize relations."

"That fellow over there would like to buy you a drink, have you refuse it, and then ask you to step outside for a moment."

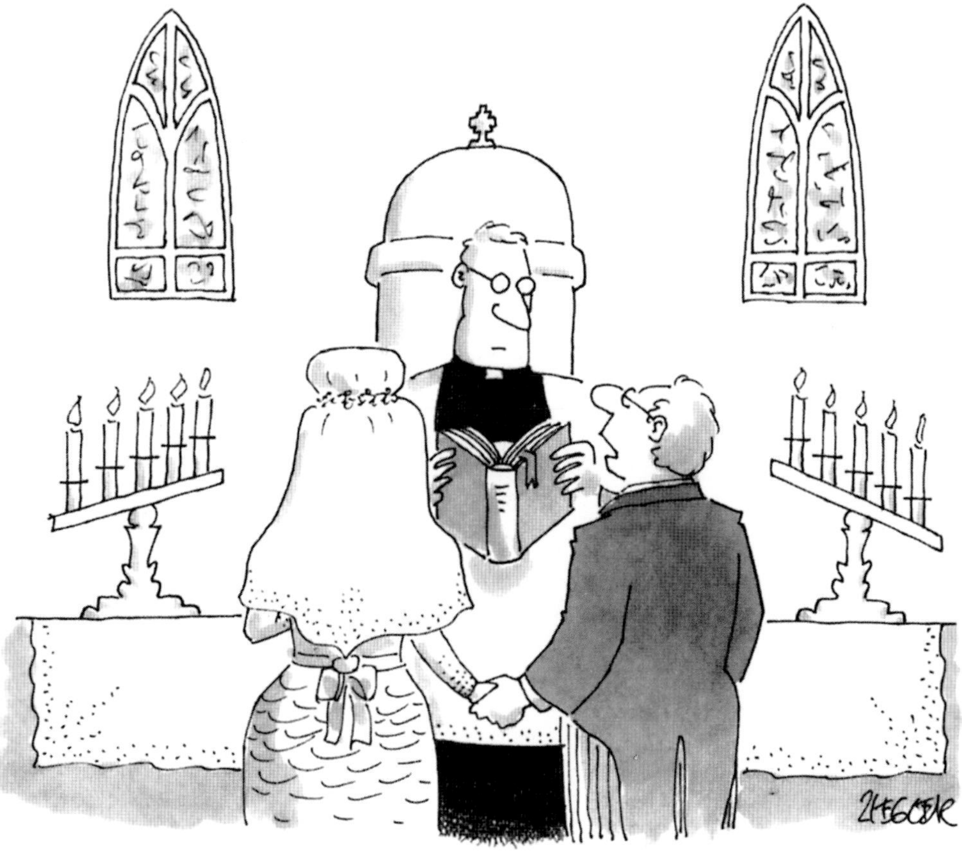
ZIEGLER

"Excuse me, Reverend, but what, exactly, do you have to do to get a drink around here?"

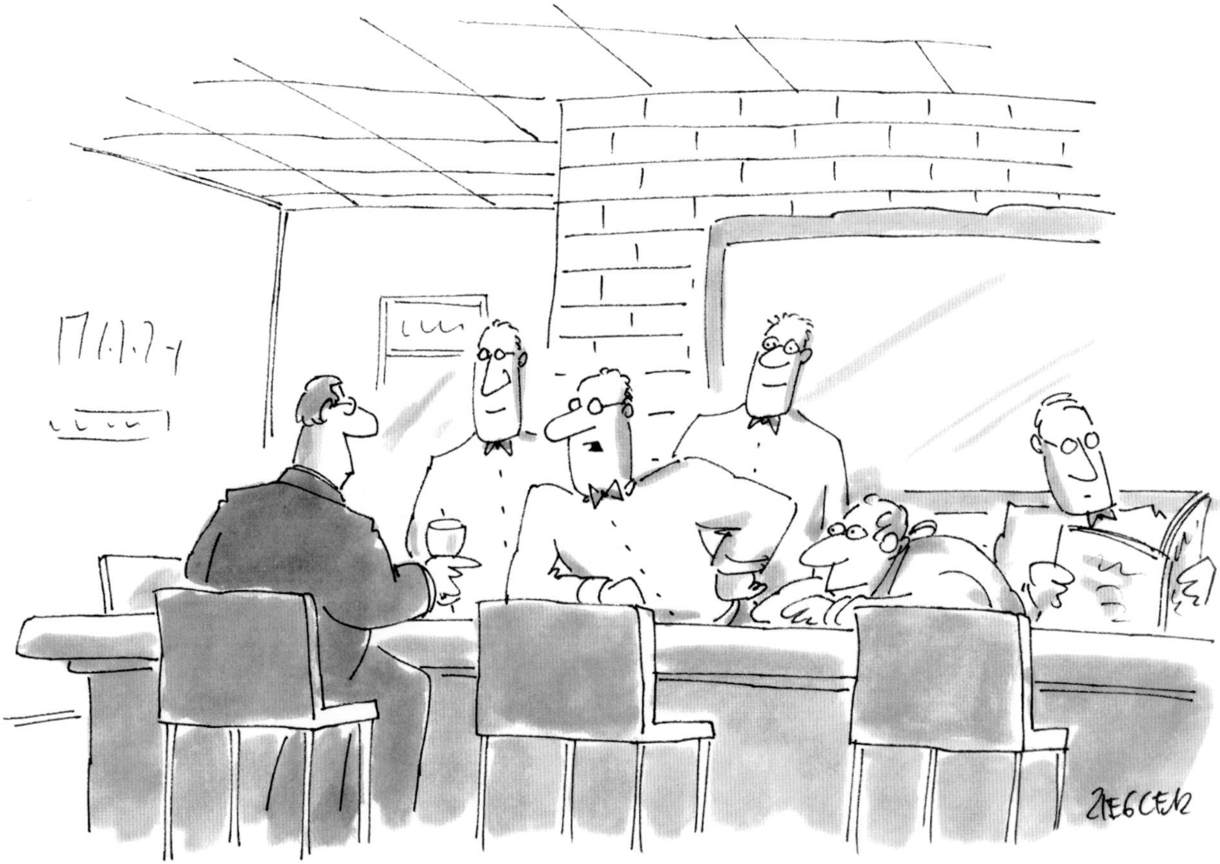
ZIEGLER

"I pour the liquor. Al does the mixers. Mack handles the beer and wine. Pete—fruits and garnishes. And Walt is our jack-of-all-trades, ready to spring to action, should one of us need to step briefly away."

"My funny valentine is no longer funny ha-ha."

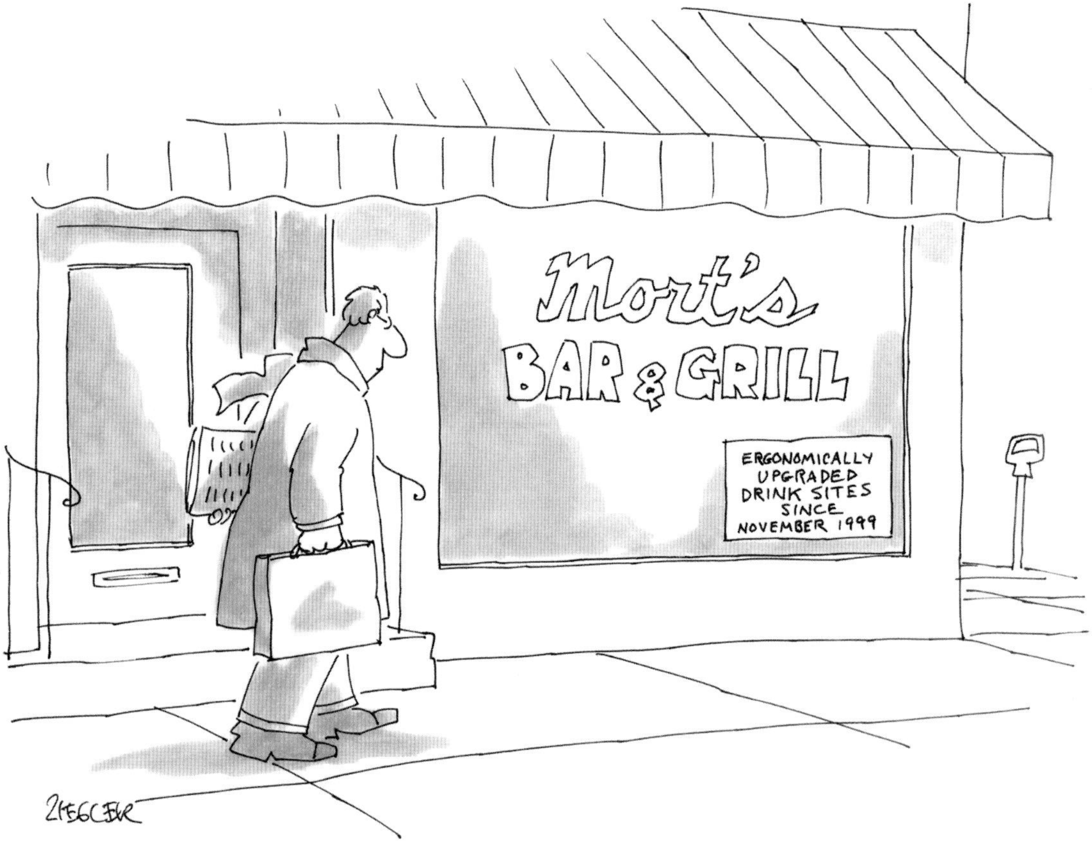
Mort's
BAR & GRILL
ERGONOMICALLY UPGRADED DRINK SITES SINCE NOVEMBER 1999
ZIEGLER

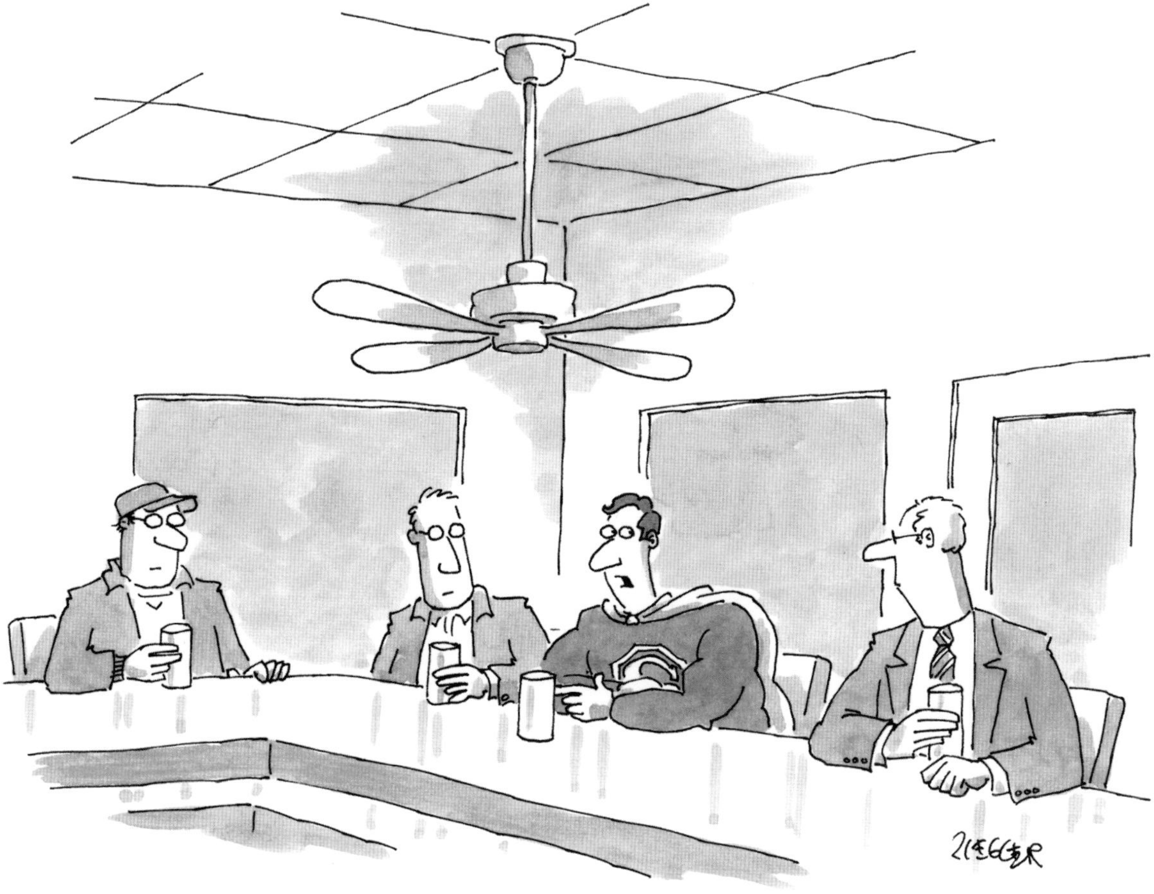
ZIEGLER

"Anybody feel like arm-wrestling for shots?"

"Excuse me, Miss, but all the wealth, might, and firepower of the United States of America would like to buy you a drink."

"When I first learned that men and women have significantly different ways of thinking, I said, 'Excellent! This calls for a drink!'"

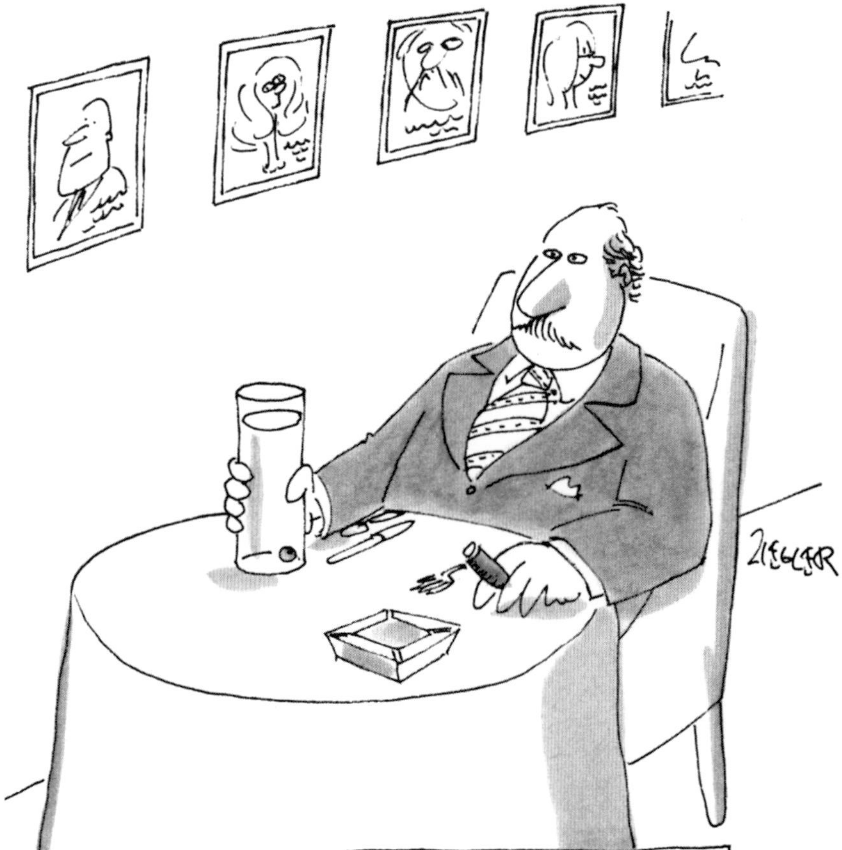
ZIEGLER

ONE-MARTINI LUNCH

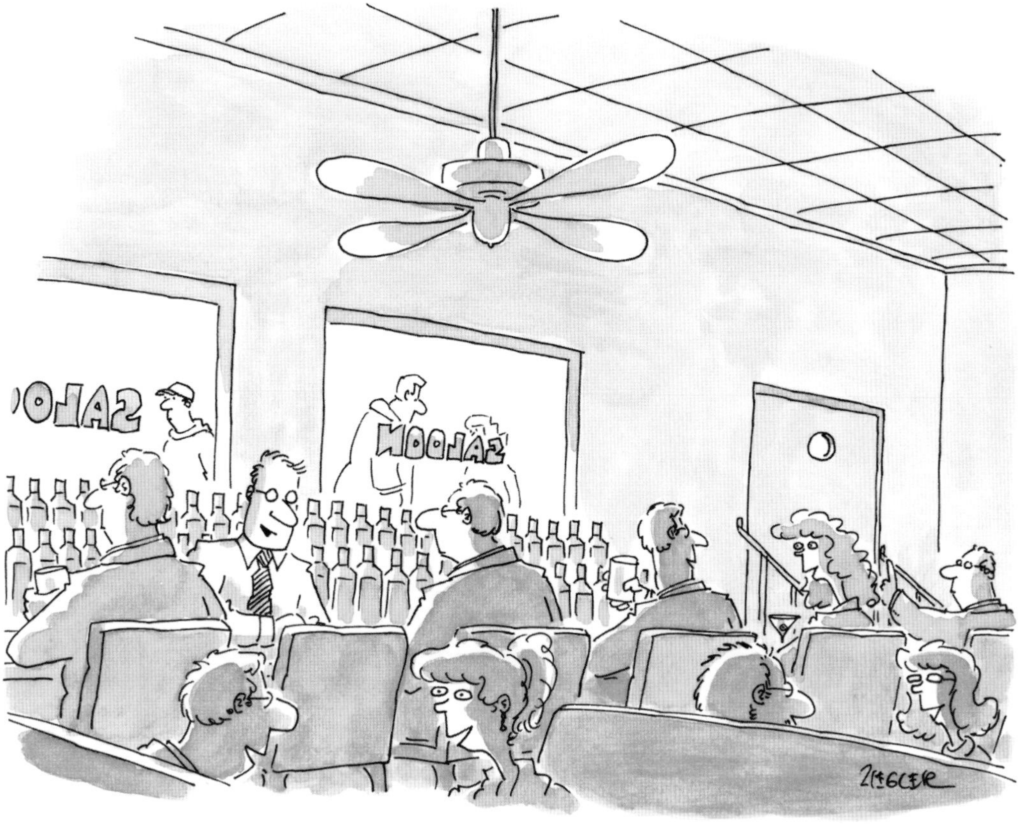
ZIEGLER

"My 401(k) is safe. It's tied up in booze futures."

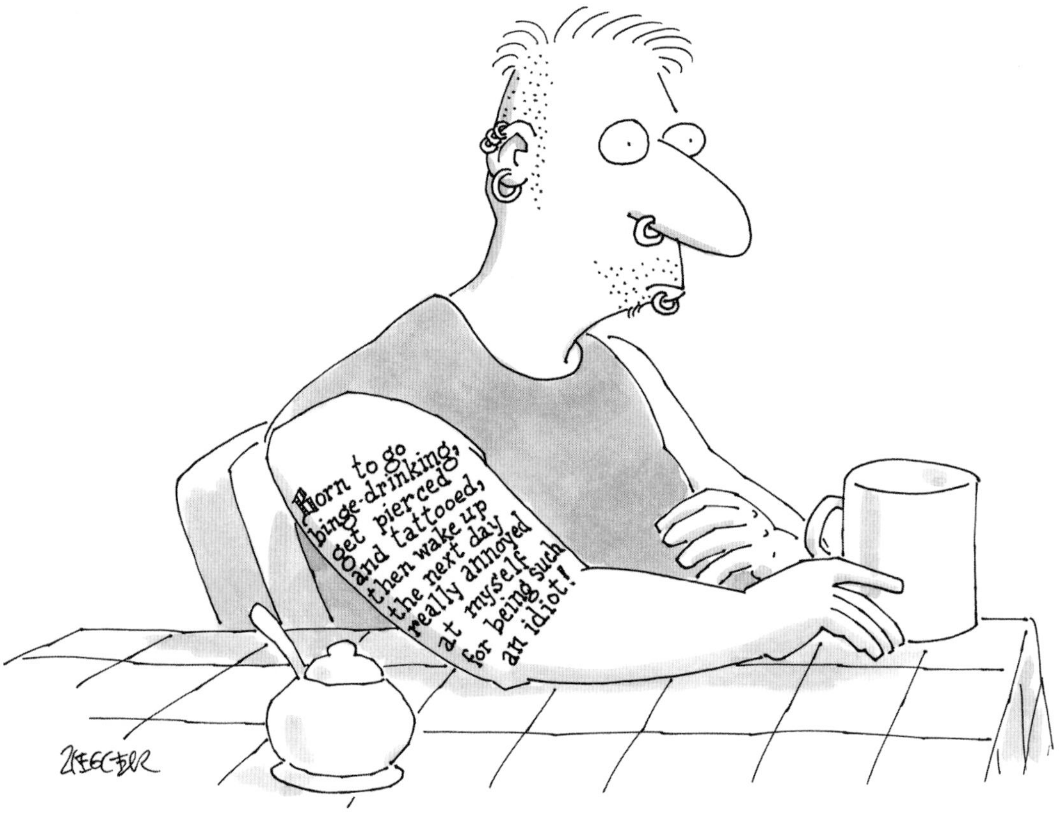
Born to go
binge-drinking,
get pierced
and tattooed,
then wake up
the next day
really annoyed
at myself
for being such
an idiot!
ZIEGLER

"*O, that we could only harness this wisdom!*"

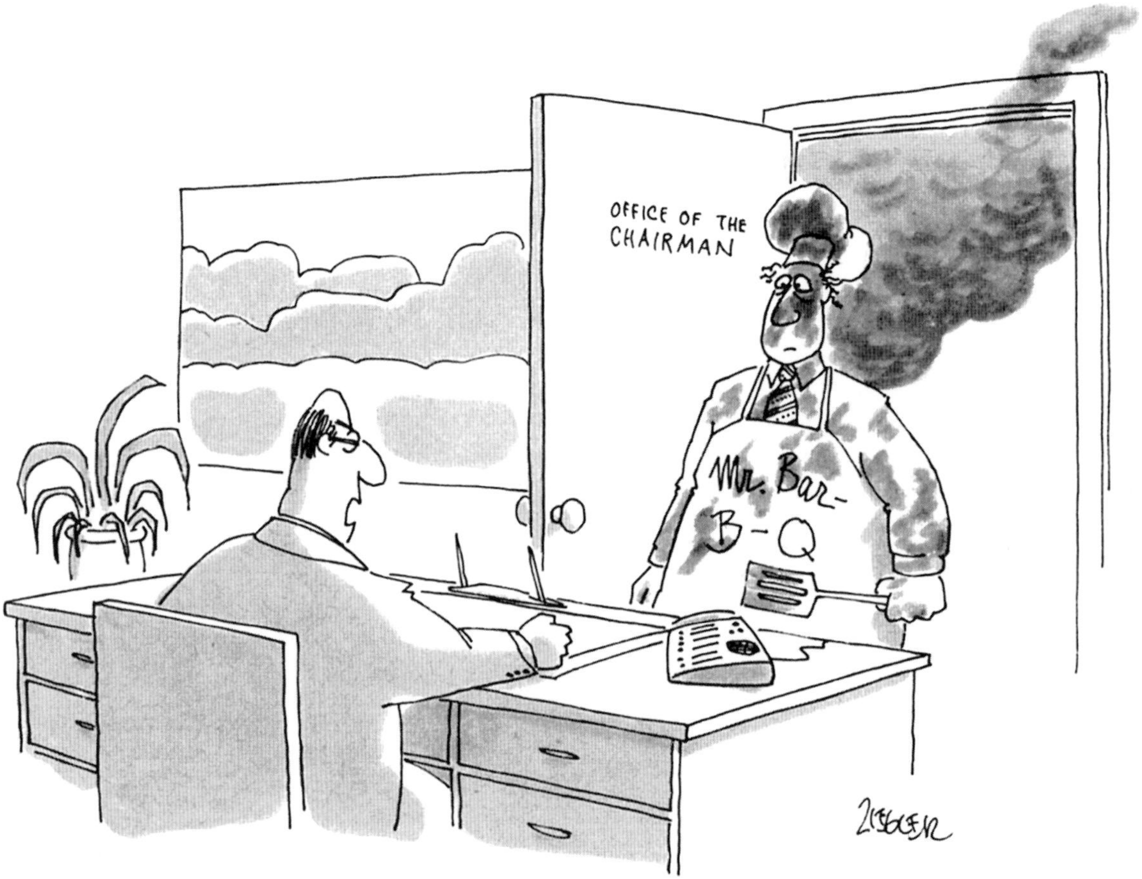
OFFICE OF THE CHAIRMAN
Mr. Bar-B-Q
ZIEGLER

"Damn it, Jacobson, why can't you go out and have yourself a three-martini lunch, like everyone else?"

EXTREME SOCIALIZING

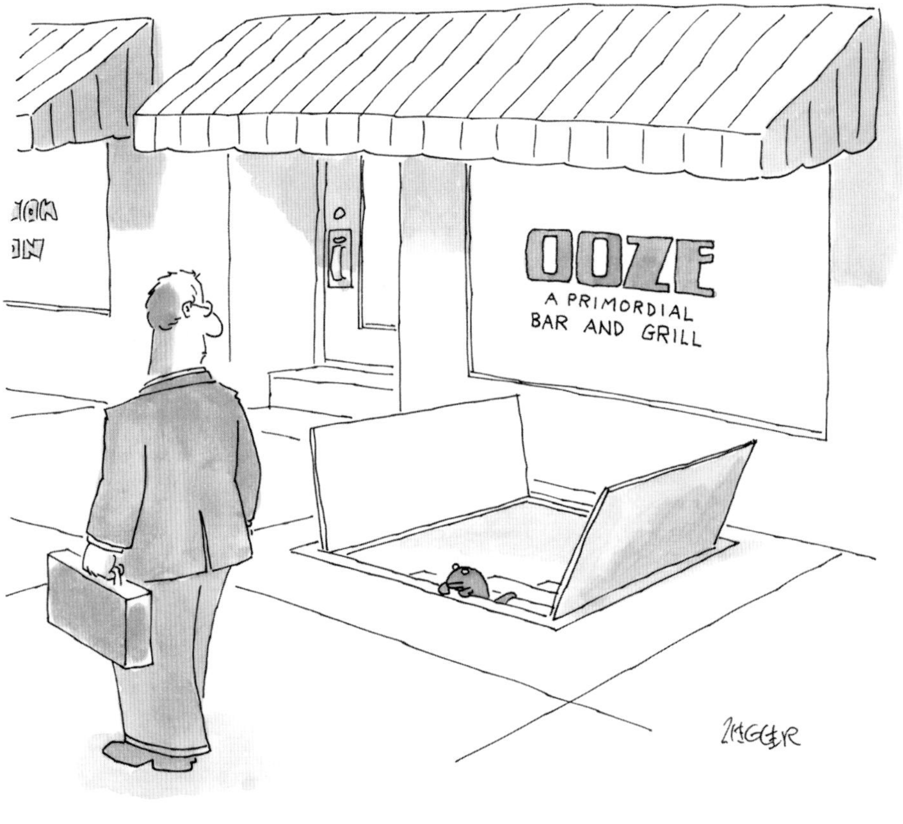
OOZE
A PRIMORDIAL
BAR AND GRILL
ZIEGLER

"O.K., you're the Roy Rogers. Who's the Shirley Temple?"

"To shuffle off this mortal coil in some saloon—it was his dream."

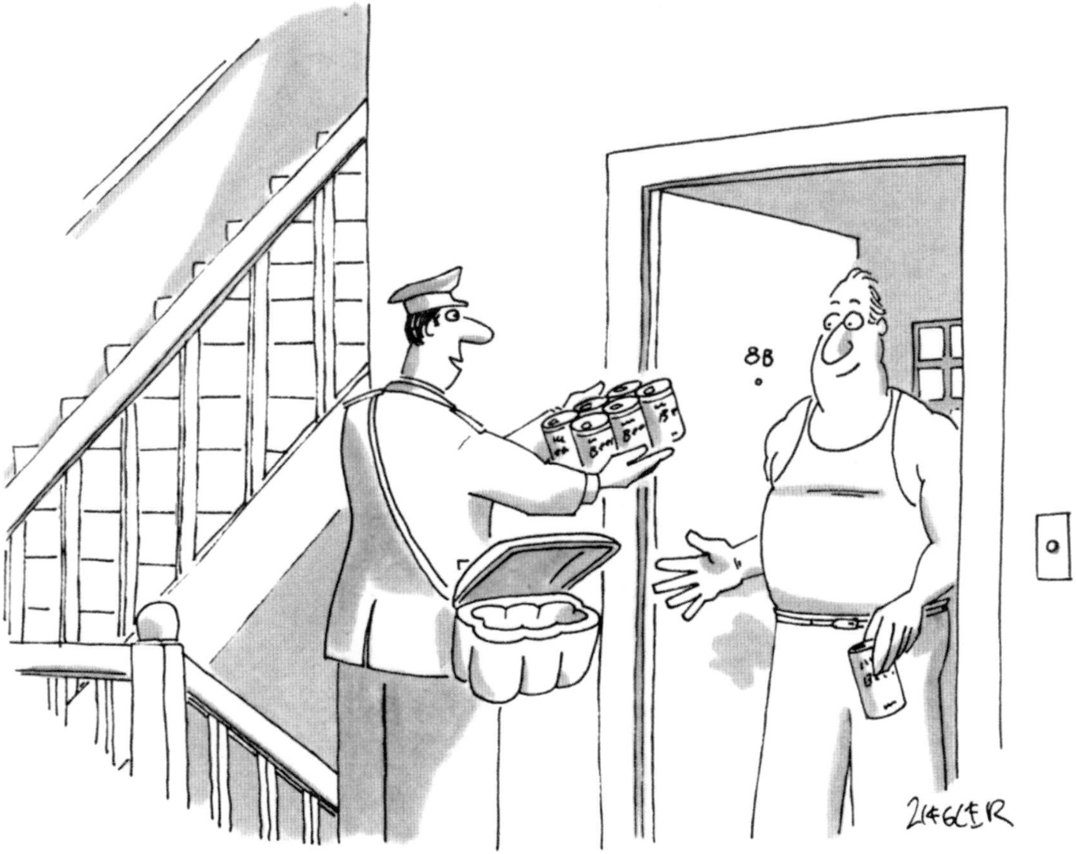
8B
ZIEGLER

"Beer-o-gram."

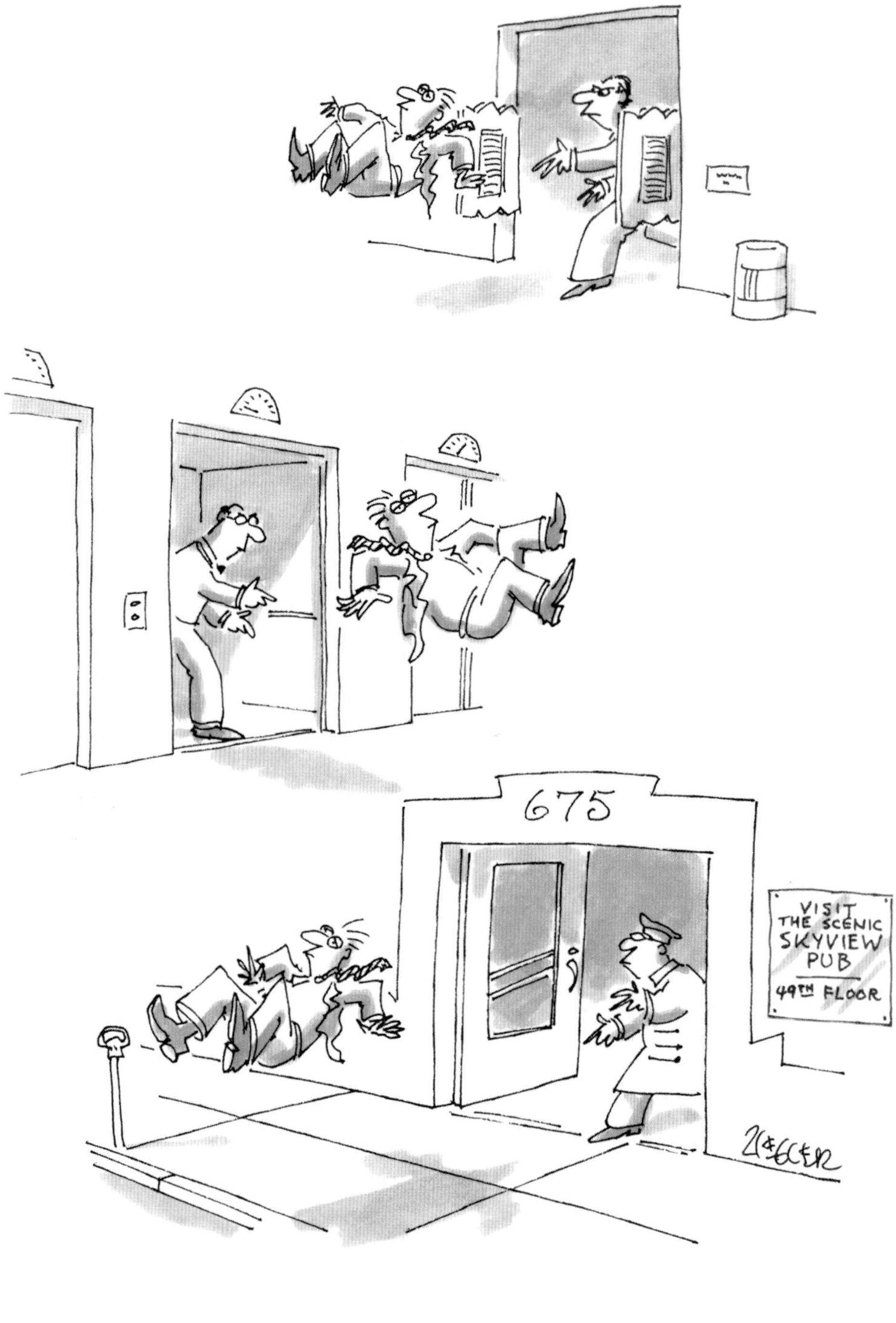
675
VISIT THE SCENIC SKYVIEW PUB
49TH FLOOR

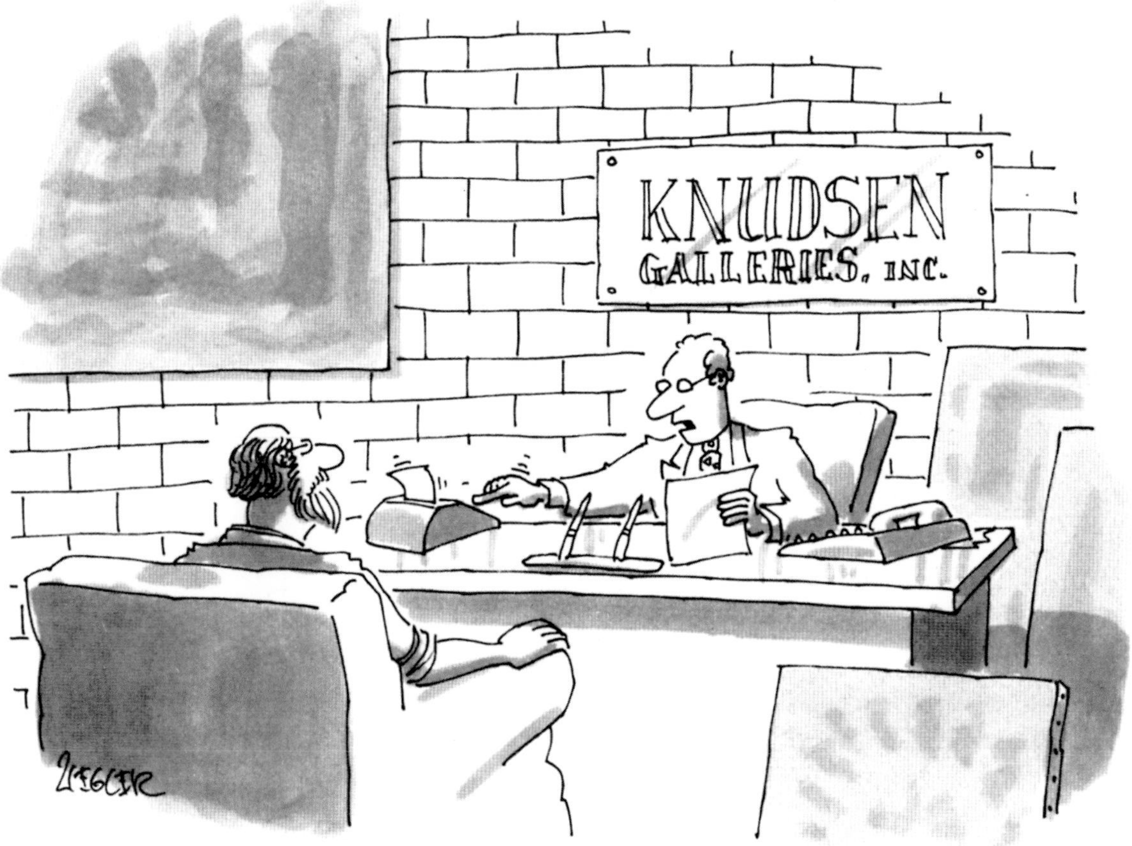
KNUDSEN
GALLERIES, INC.

"At your opening, I see that you had two glasses of wine, eight pieces of cheddar, eight crackers, and seventeen grapes. That, of course, will have to come off the top of your end."

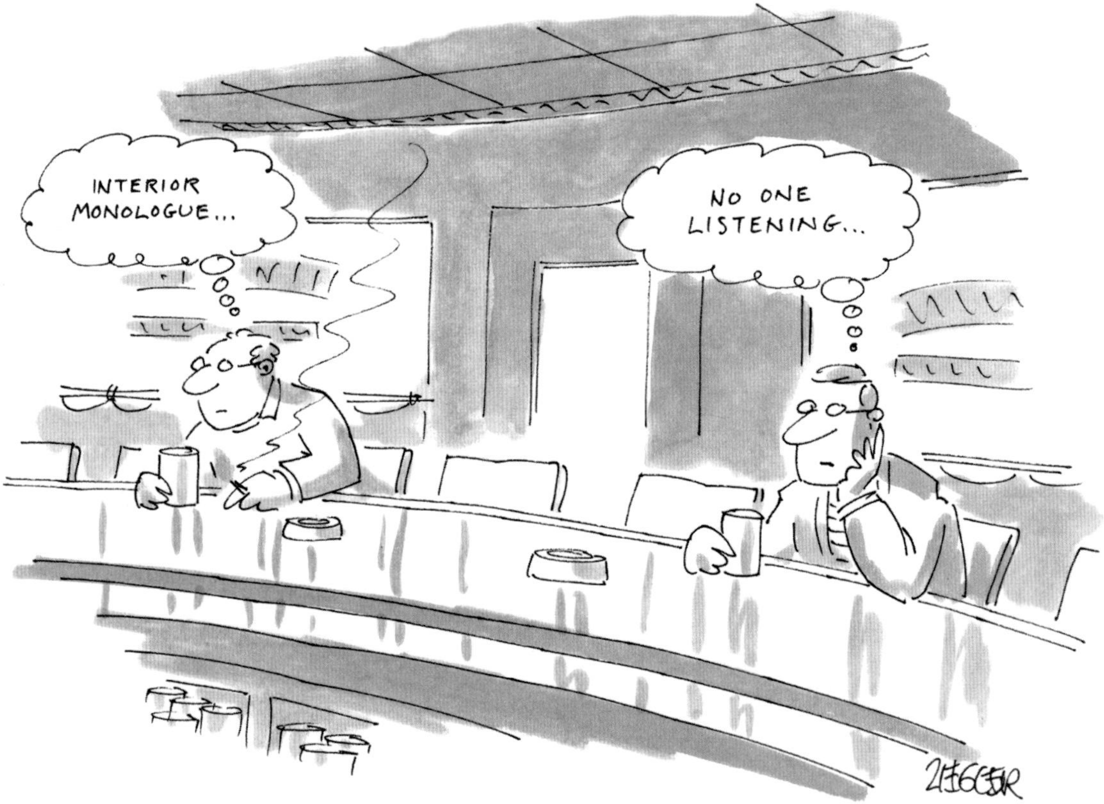
INTERIOR MONOLOGUE...
NO ONE LISTENING...
ZIEGLER

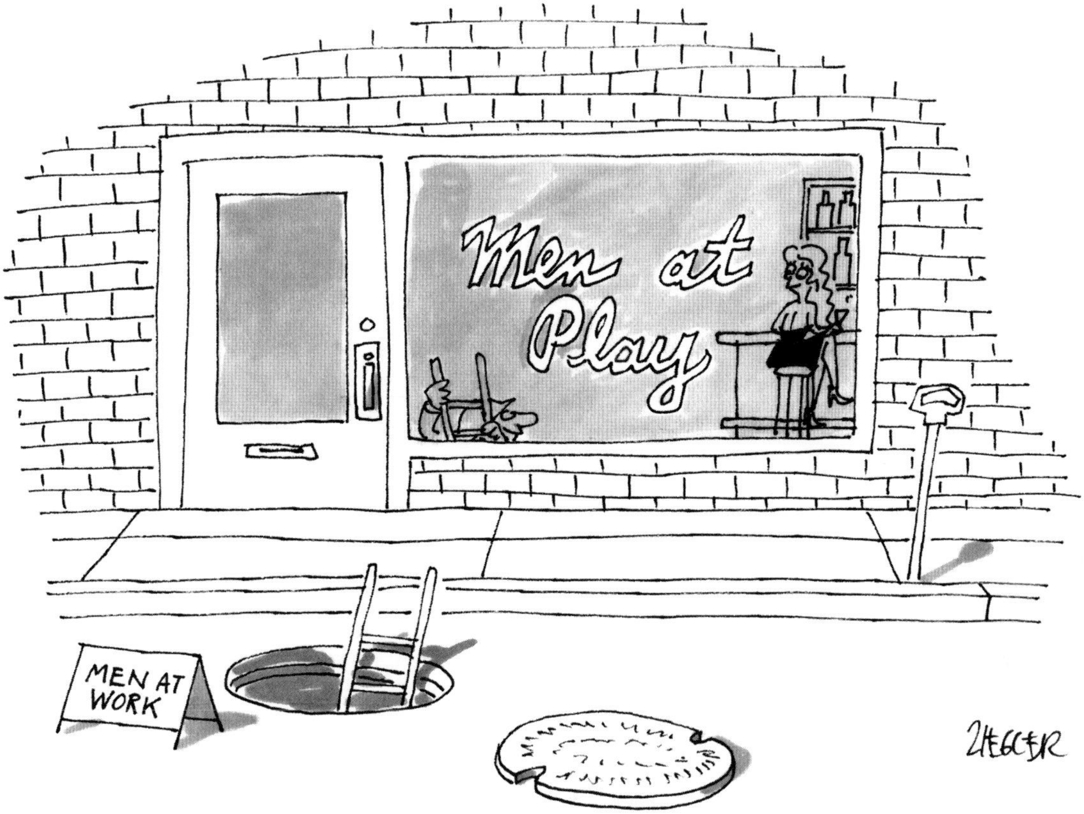
Men at Play
MEN AT WORK
ZIEGLER

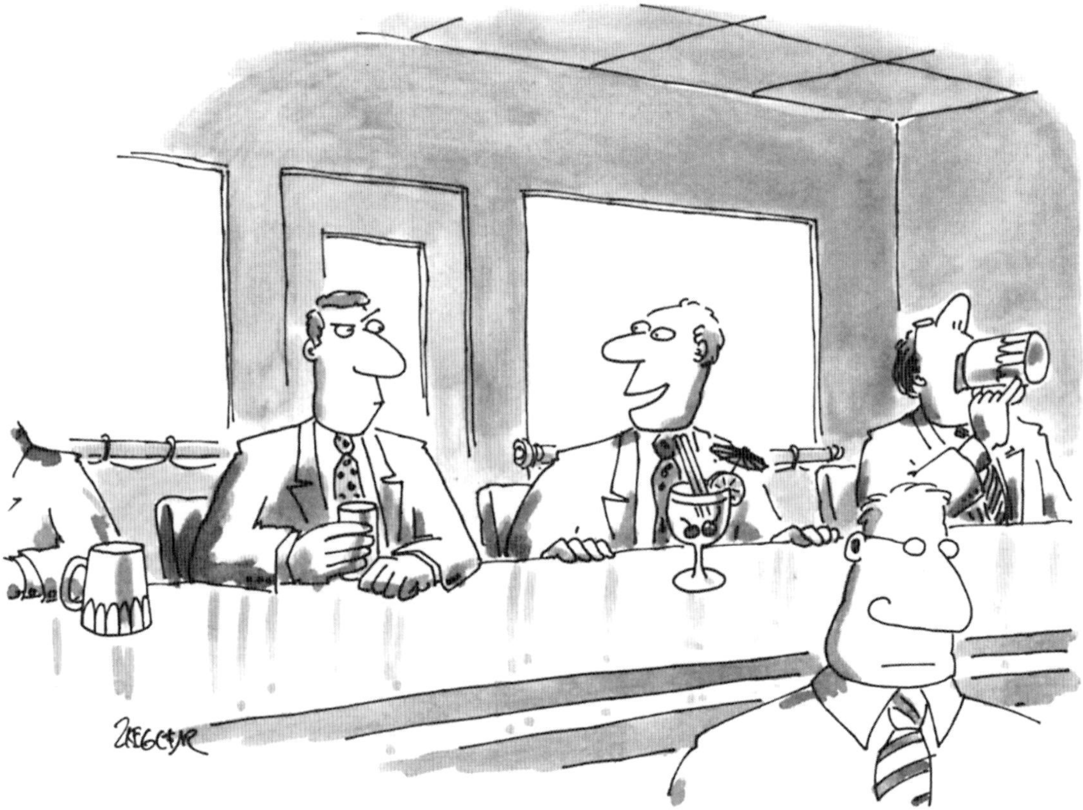
ZIEGLER

"Sipsies?"

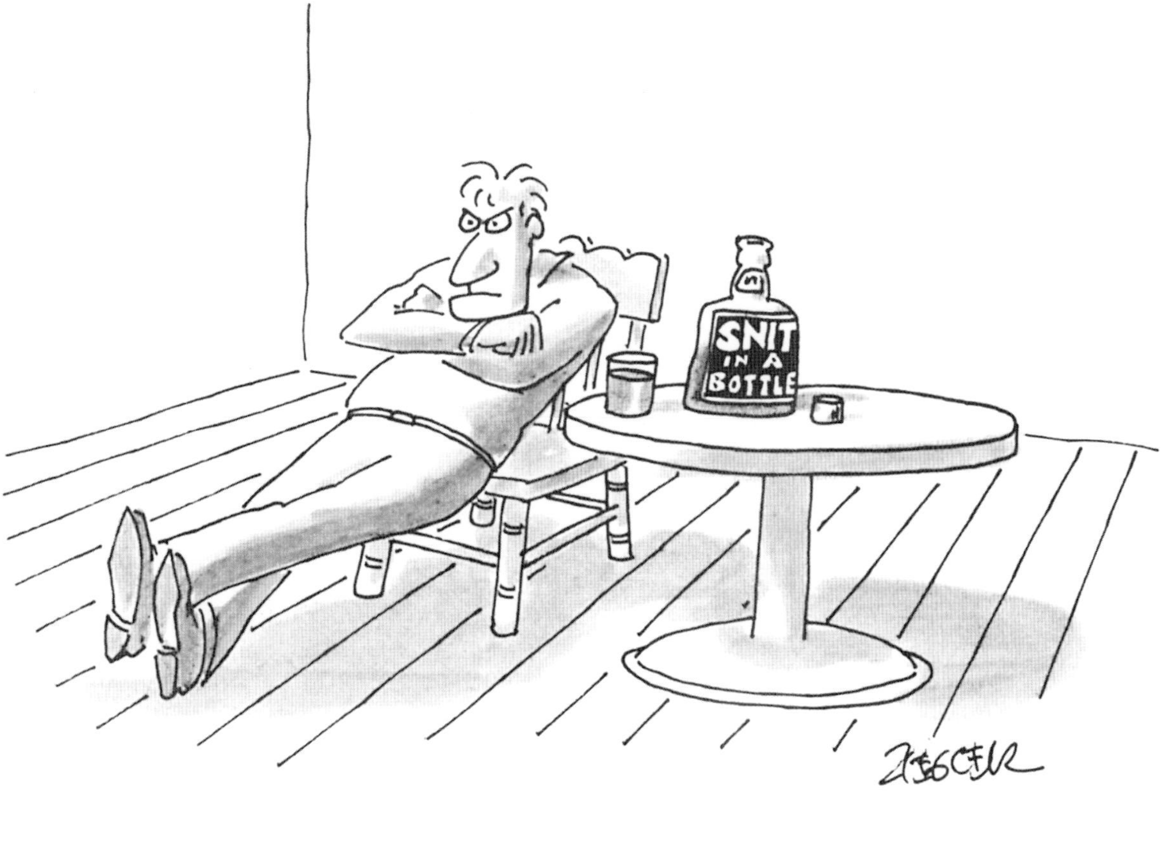
SNIT
IN A
BOTTLE

"*The ninth circle isn't so bad. I've heard there are little bowls of Cheez-Its at the bar.*"

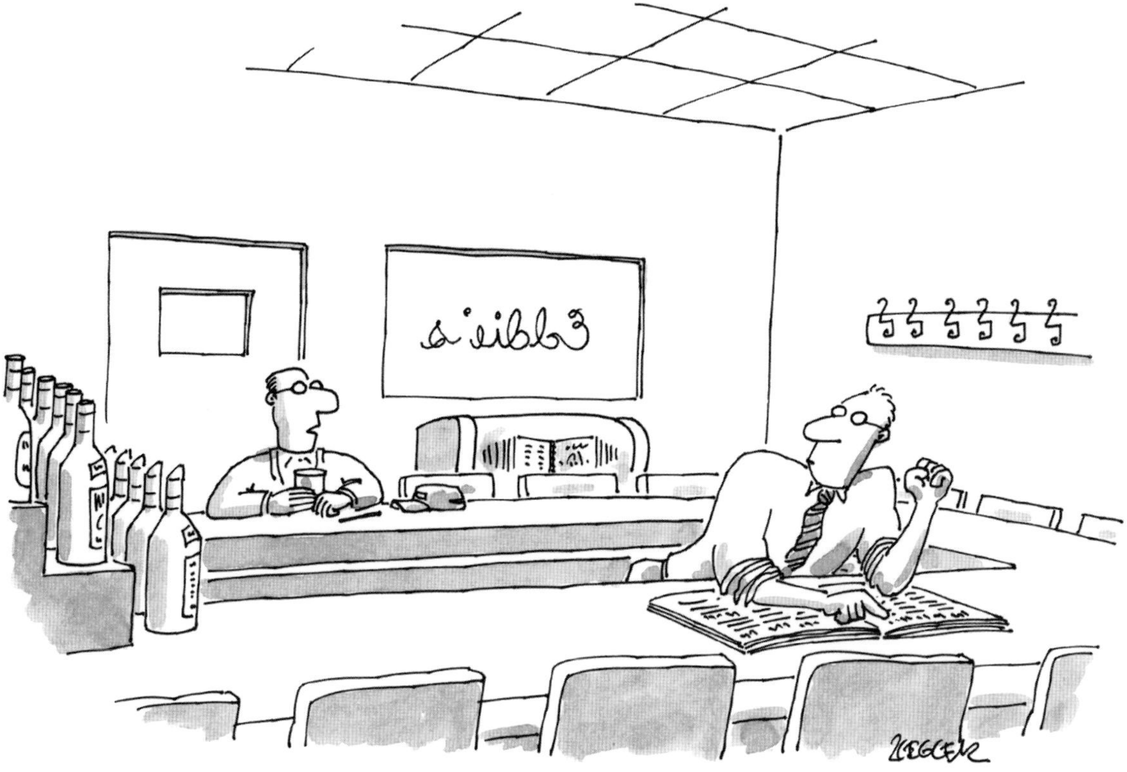
ZIEGLER

"To avoid the tedium of this endless socializing, Eddie, I have decided, beginning Monday, to obtain all my future booze from Amazon.com."

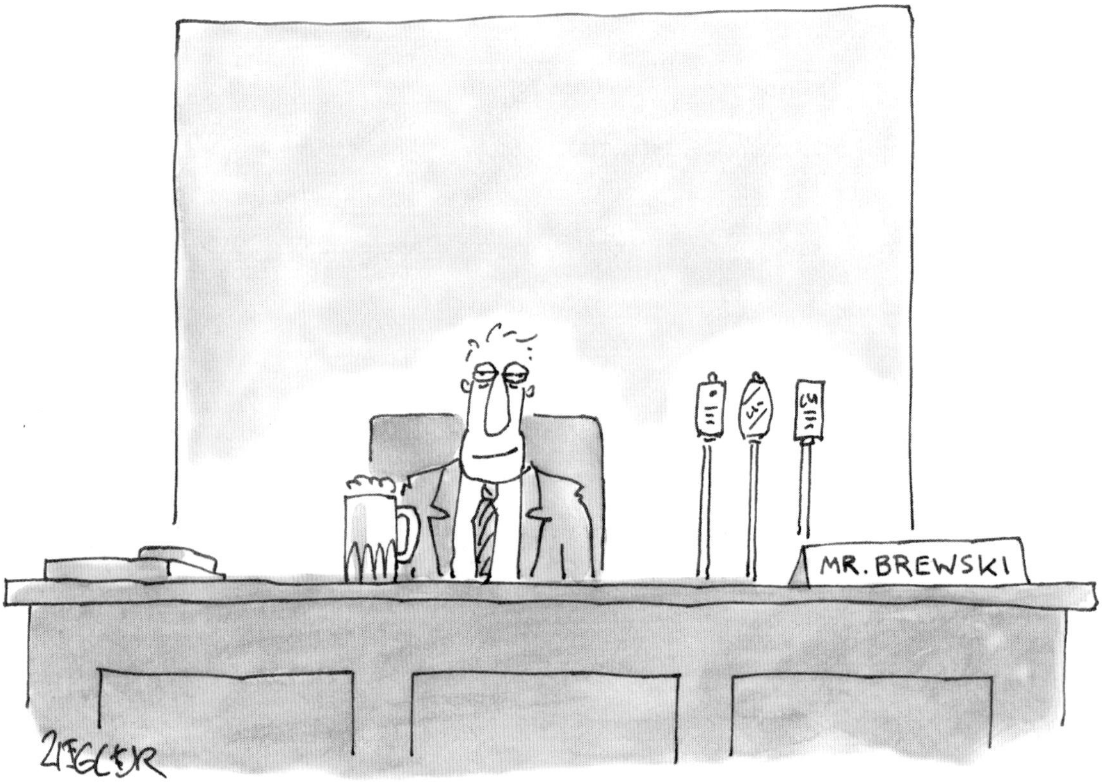
MR. BREWSKI
ZIEGLER

"Being an accountant gives him that extra aura of danger."

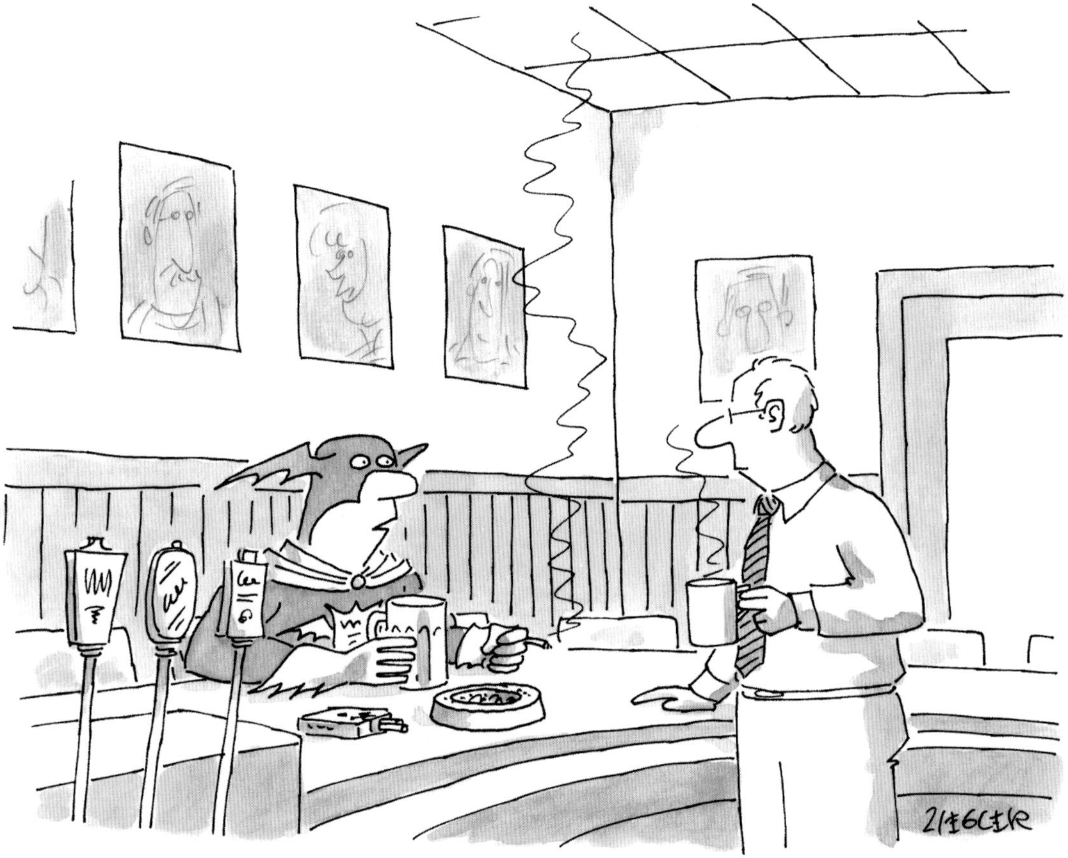
ZIEGLER

"The damsel-in-distress thing is just one of several income streams that I pursue."

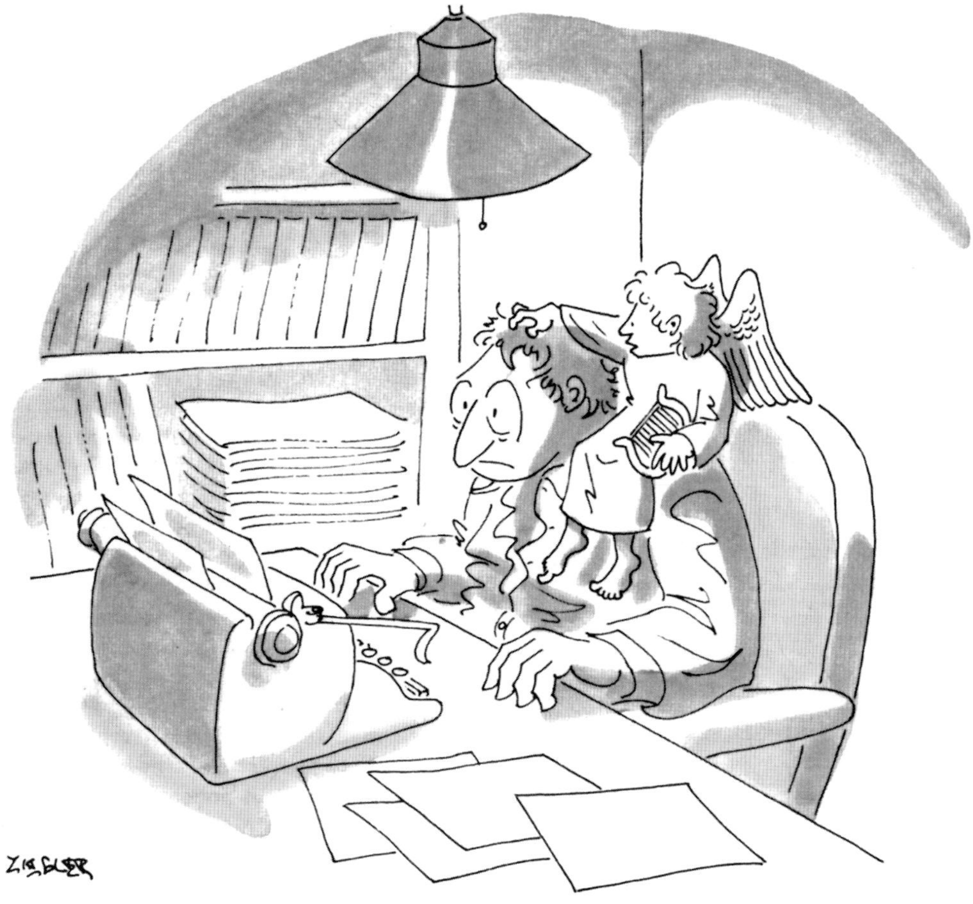
ZIEGLER

"Hey, I'm thirsty. I need a drink. A drink and a liverwurst sandwich. Hey, how about a sandwich and a beer down at Gallagher's, and then we can go shoot some pool? Or maybe take in a movie. Hey, I'm talking to you."

"All razz. No ma tazz."

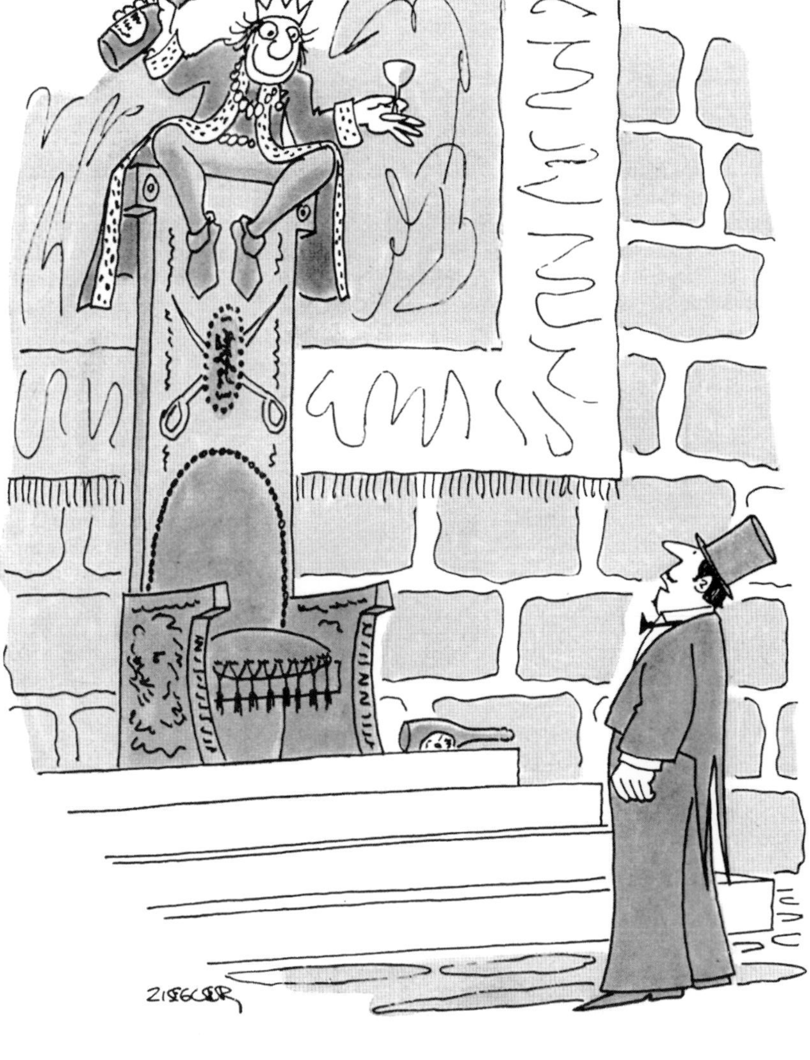
ZIEGLER

"But the people, *Your Majesty! The* people *are not happy."*

"*Here's to East, West, South, and Bridgehampton, and all the little Hamptons in between.*"

"Don't get me wrong, Ted. I like you, but you're not a special person. I'm a special person."

"*It is fun being French, is it not, Henri?*"

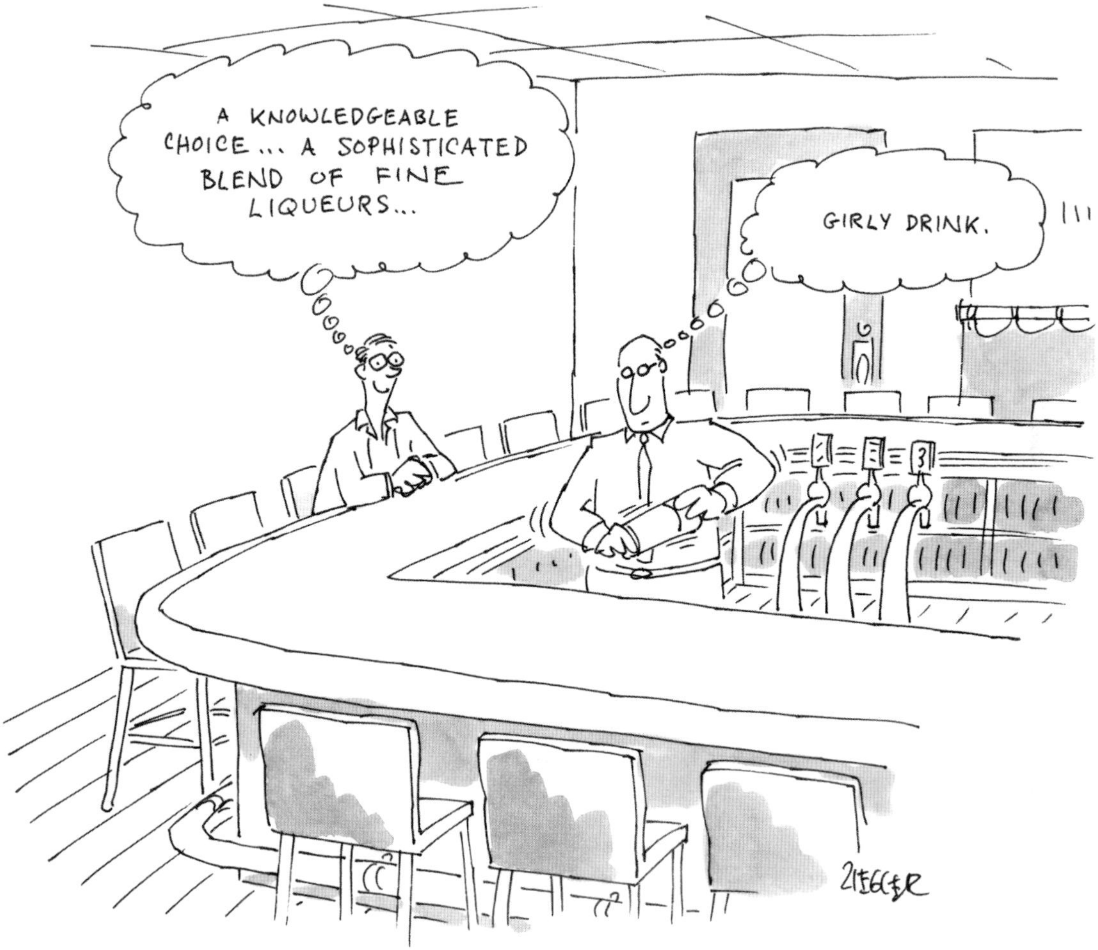
A KNOWLEDGEABLE CHOICE... A SOPHISTICATED BLEND OF FINE LIQUEURS...
GIRLY DRINK.
ZIEGLER

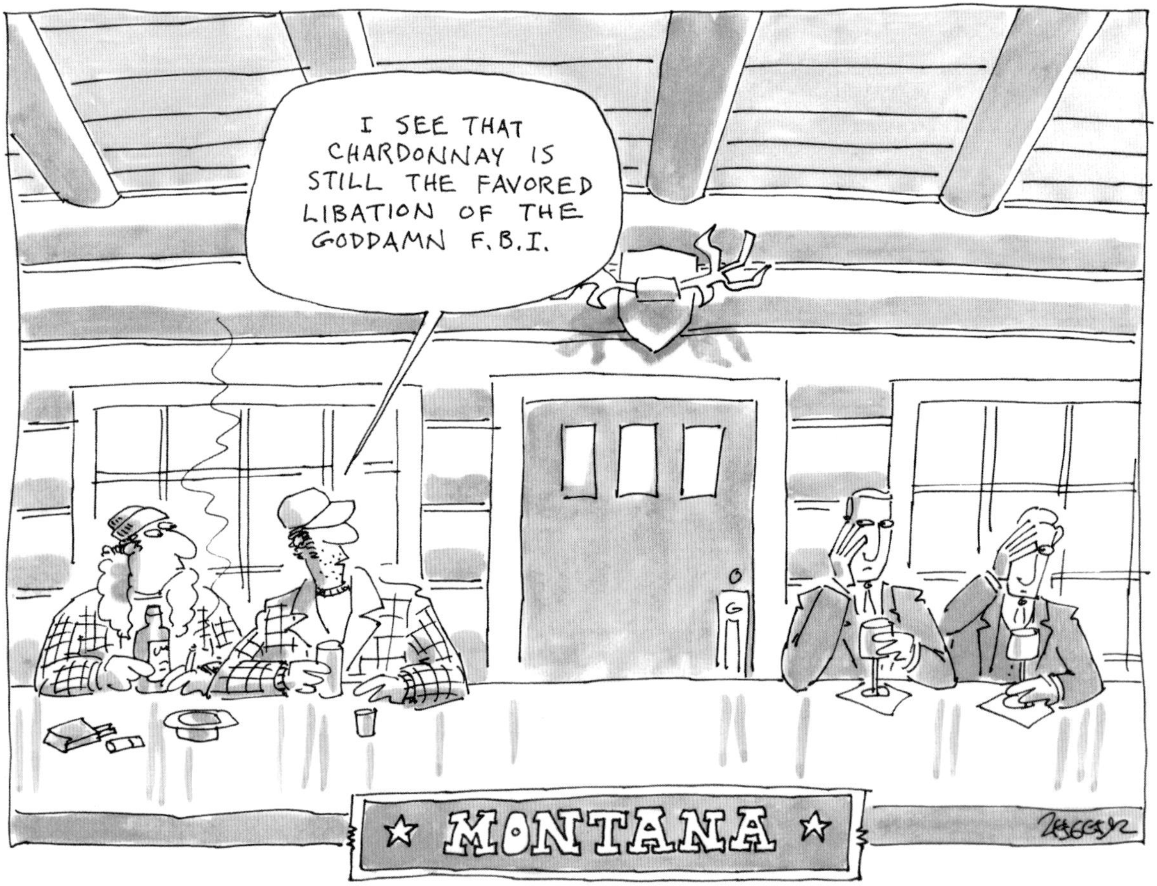
I SEE THAT CHARDONNAY IS STILL THE FAVORED LIBATION OF THE GODDAMN F.B.I.
MONTANA

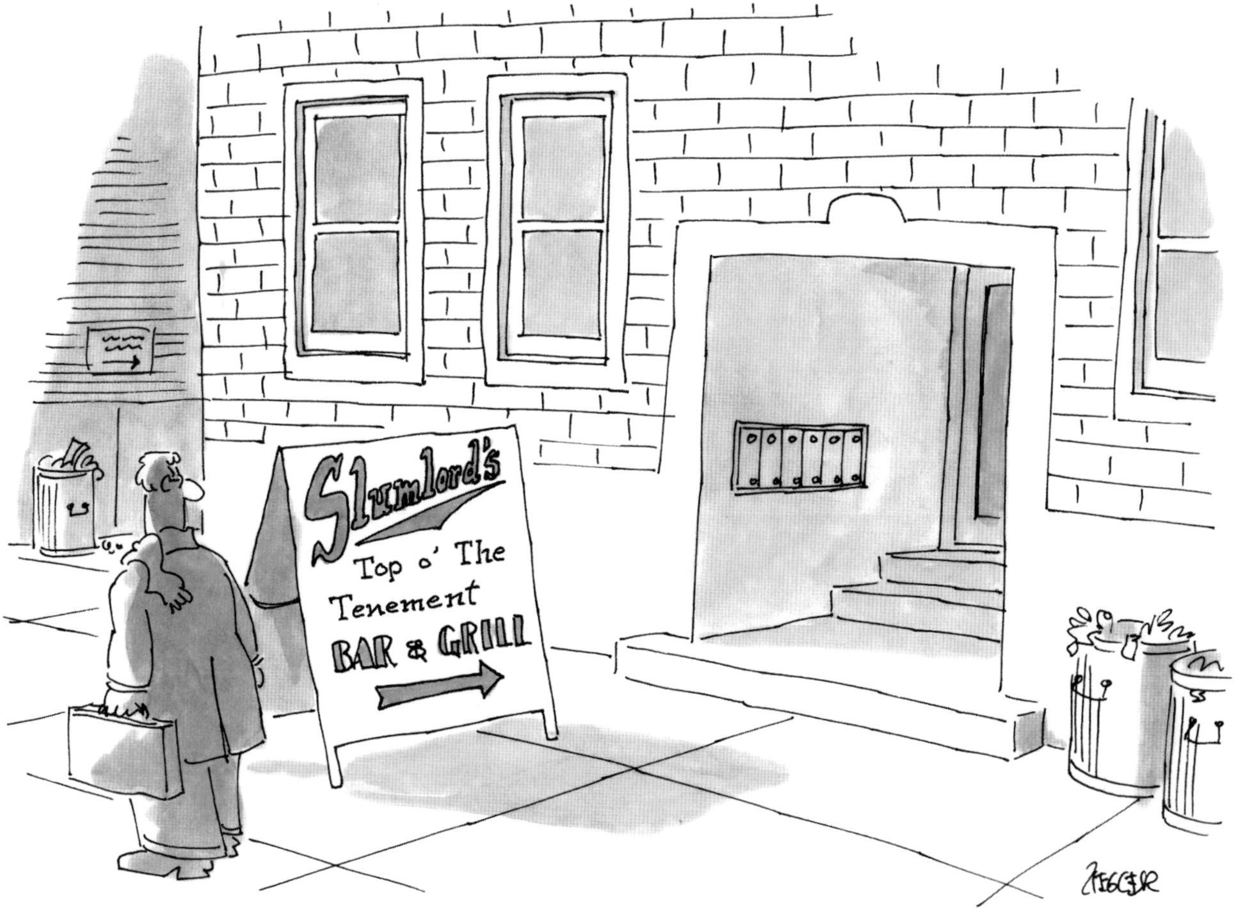
Slumlord's
Top o' The
Tenement
BAR & GRILL

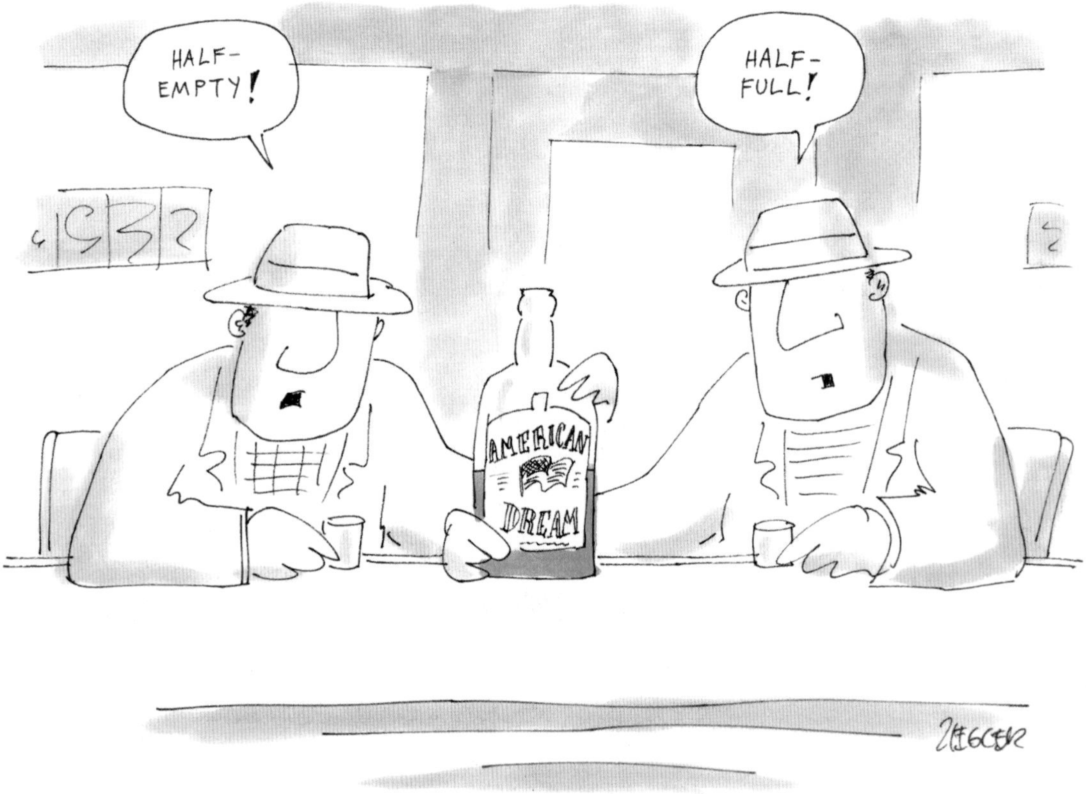
HALF-EMPTY!
HALF-FULL!
AMERICAN DREAM
ZIEGLER

"The shirt, kerchief, and pants—all Ralph Lauren. The belt and my undergarments—Calvin Klein."

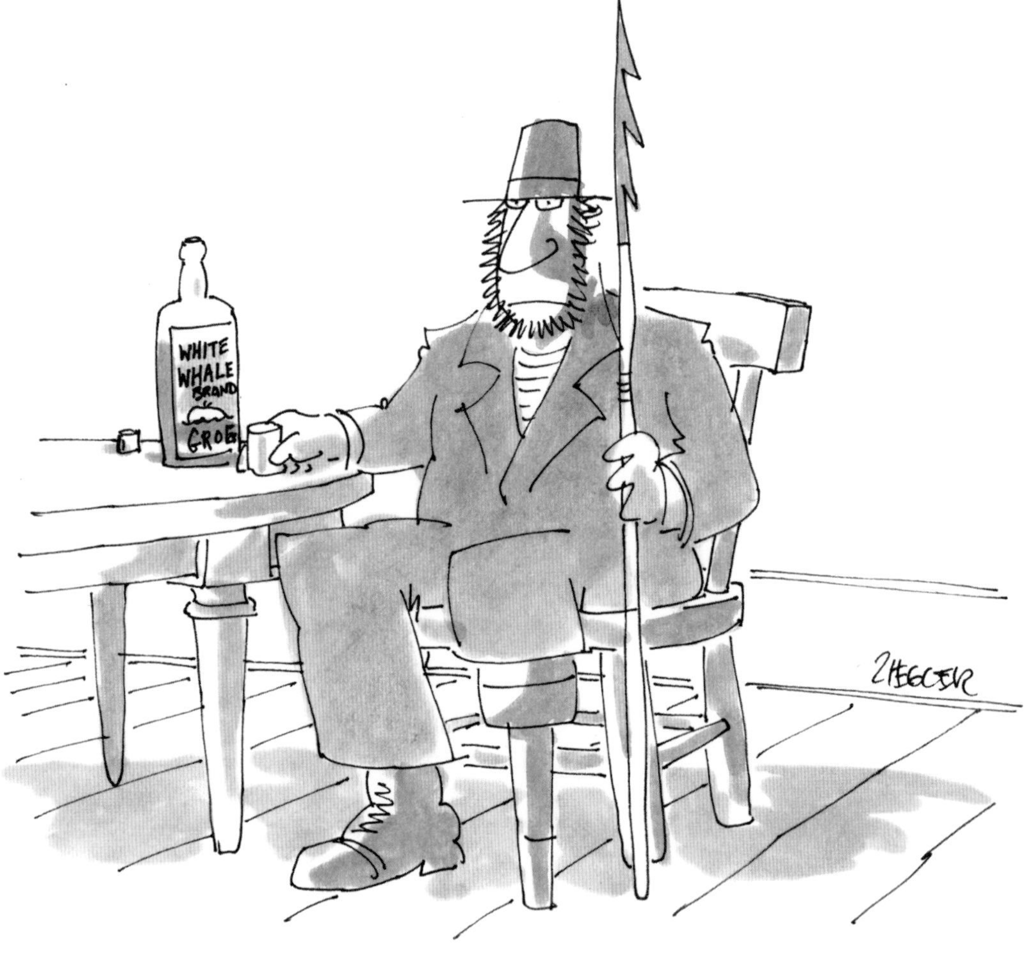
WHITE
WHALE
BRAND
GROG

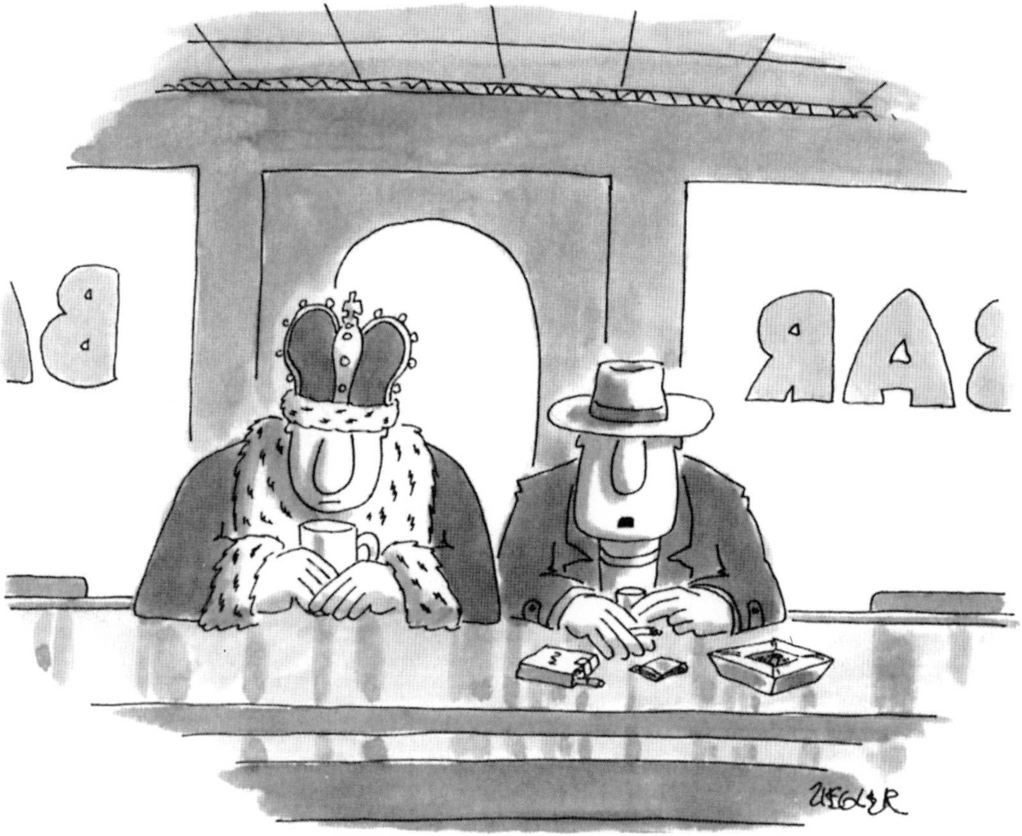
ZIEGLER

"Why is it that the people in charge always turn out to be idiots? Present company, of course, excepted."

"Careful. Straw in drink is closer than it actually appears."

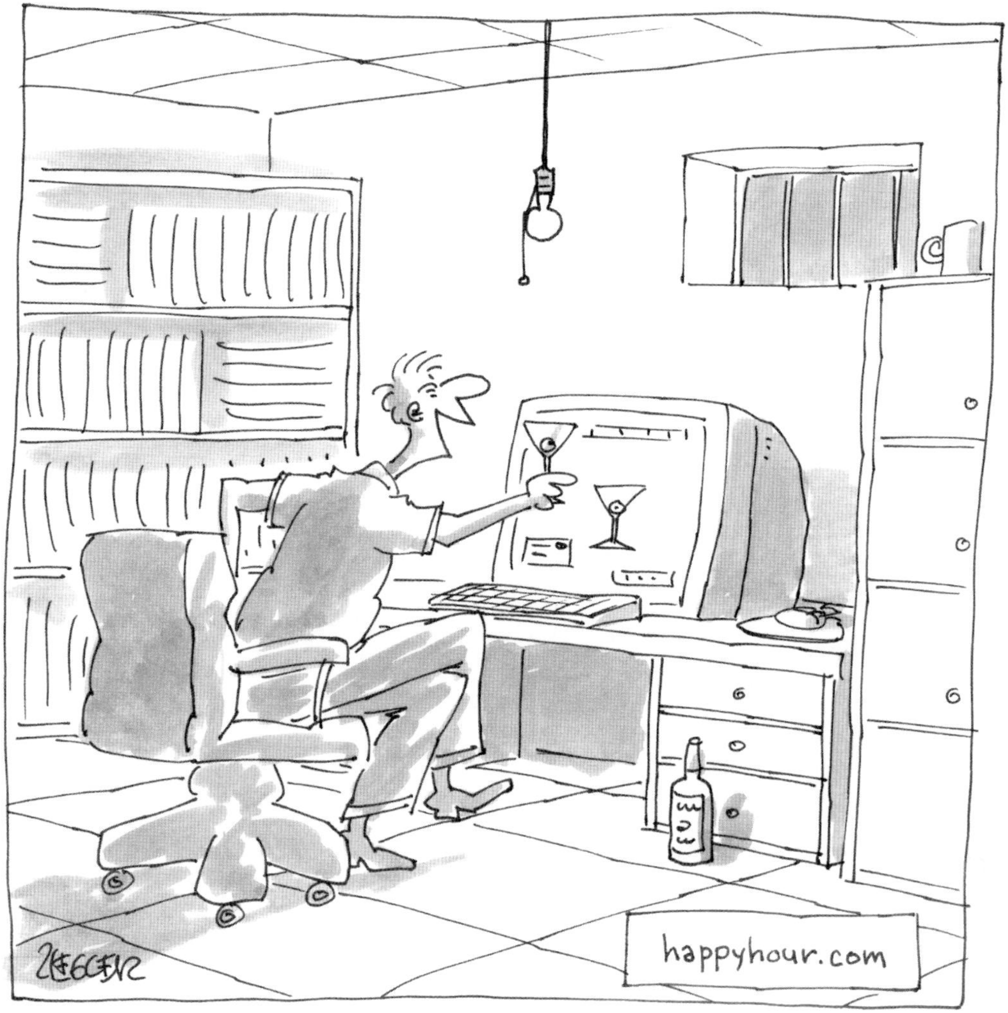
ZIEGLER

happyhour.com

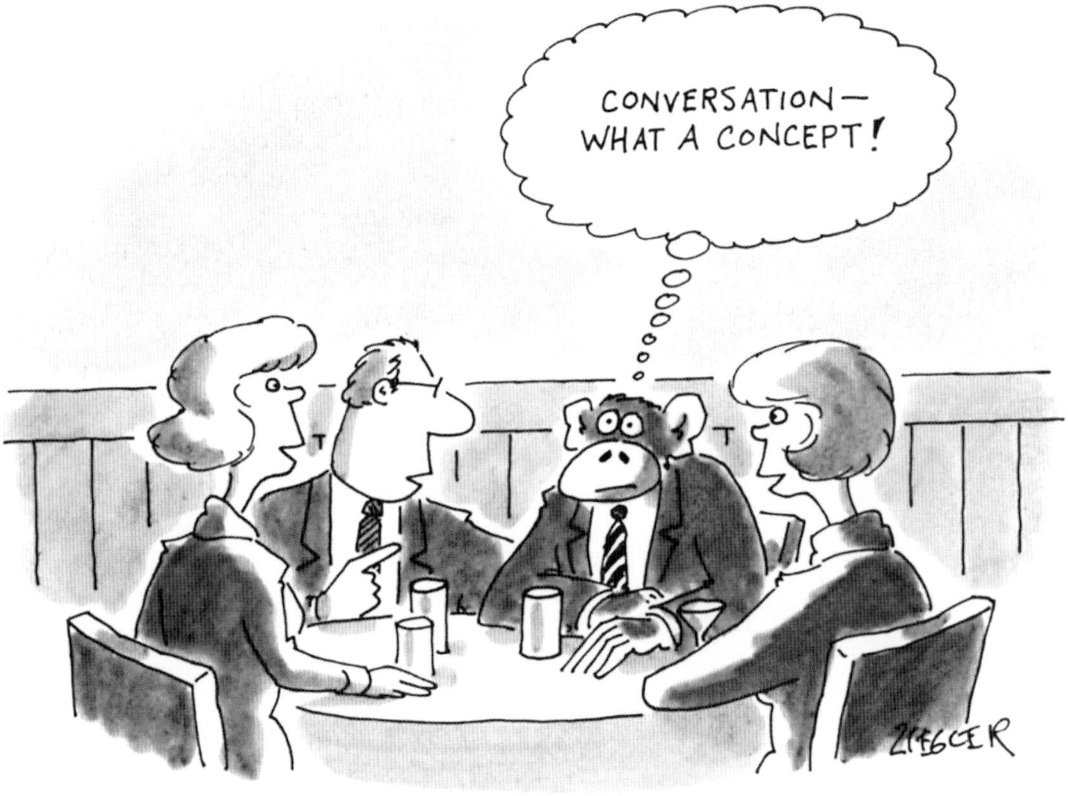
CONVERSATION—
WHAT A CONCEPT!
ZIEGLER

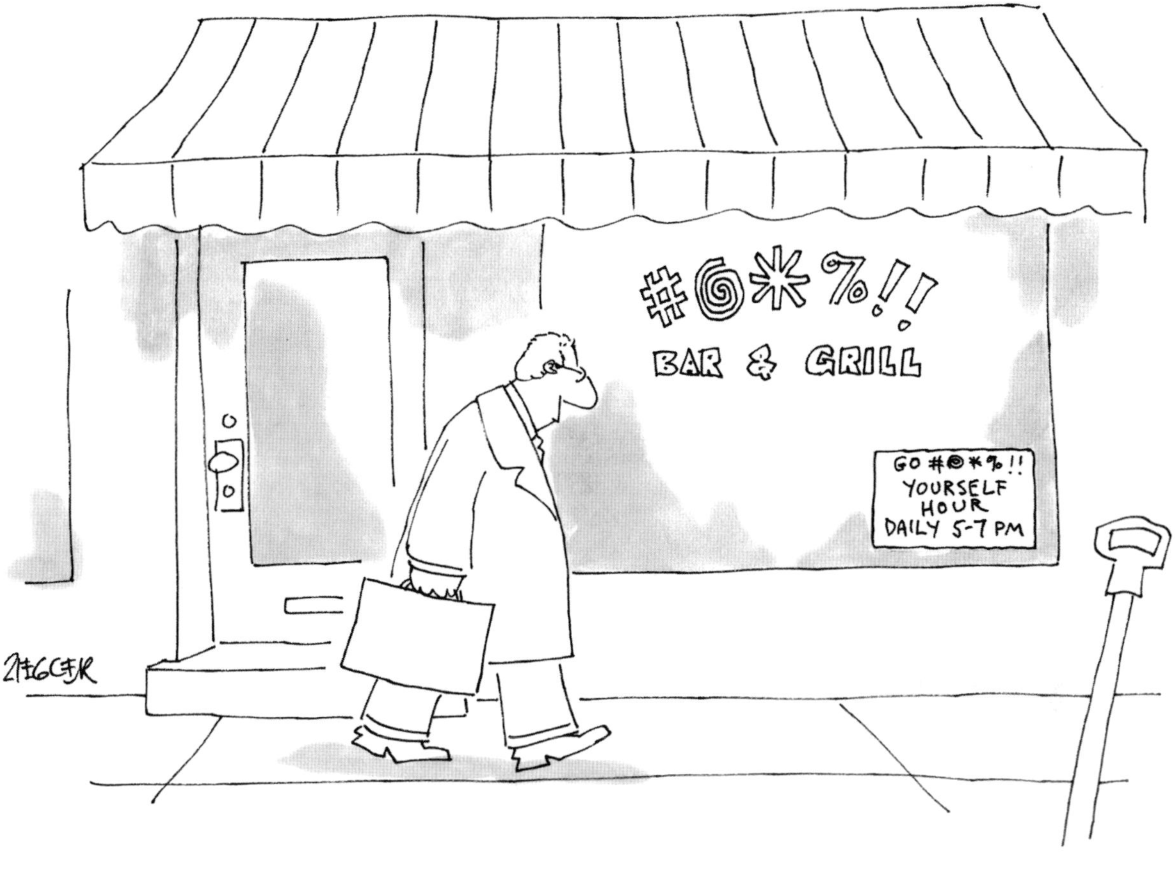
#@*%!!
BAR & GRILL
GO #@*%!! YOURSELF HOUR DAILY 5-7 PM
ZIEGLER

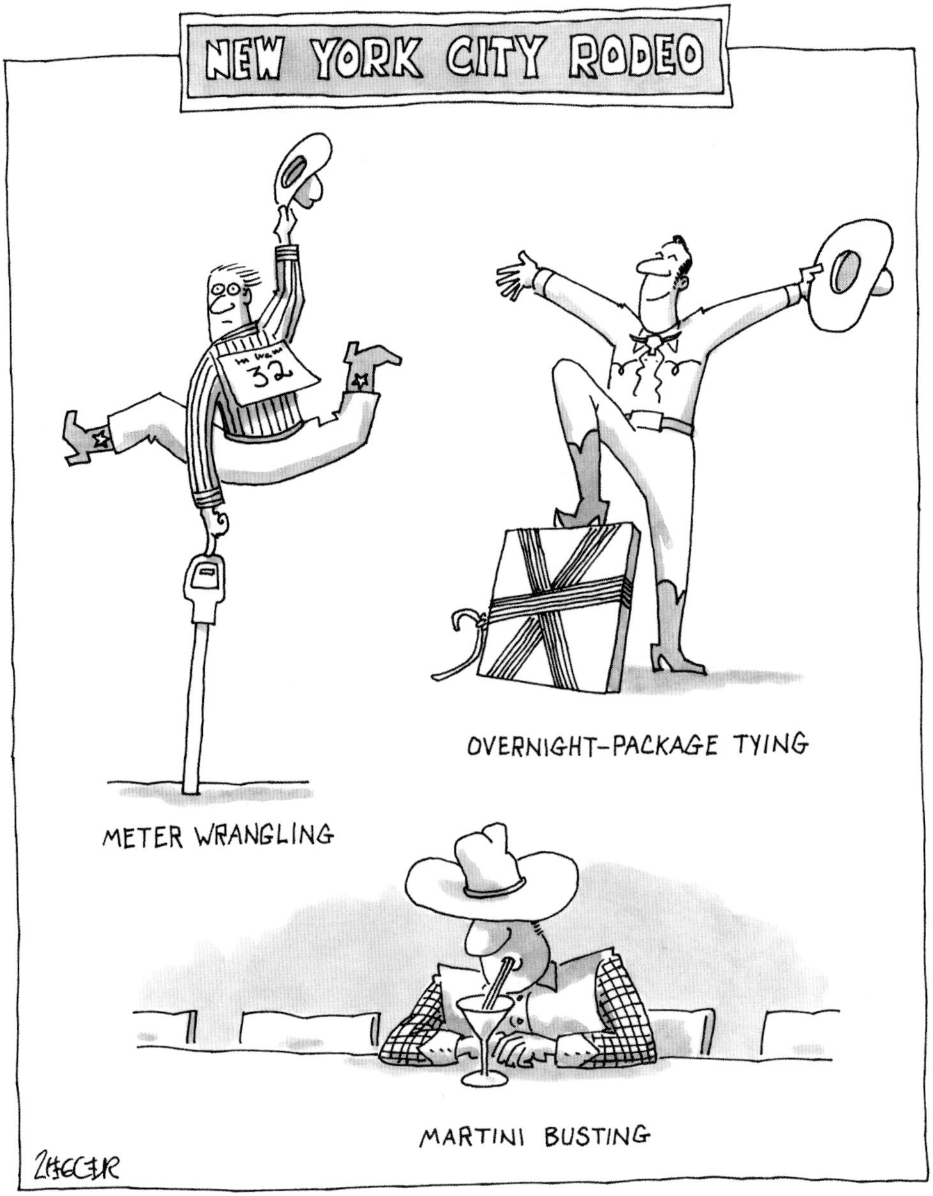
NEW YORK CITY RODEO
32
METER WRANGLING
OVERNIGHT-PACKAGE TYING
MARTINI BUSTING
ZIEGLER

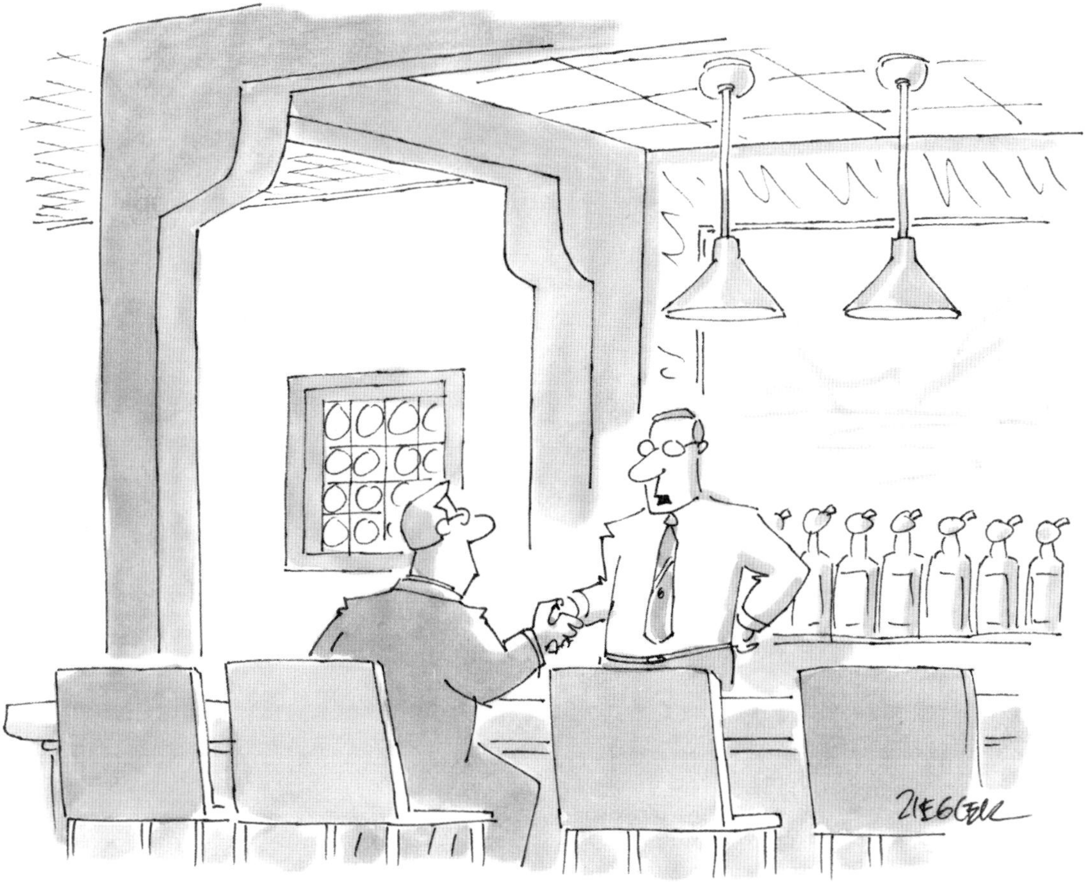
ZIEGLER

"Long time no see, Mr. Jimmy. I understand congratulations are in order on your recent engagement, wedding, and divorce."

"Hey, pal, let's hear 'Doggie in the Window' again, and this time play it like you mean it!"

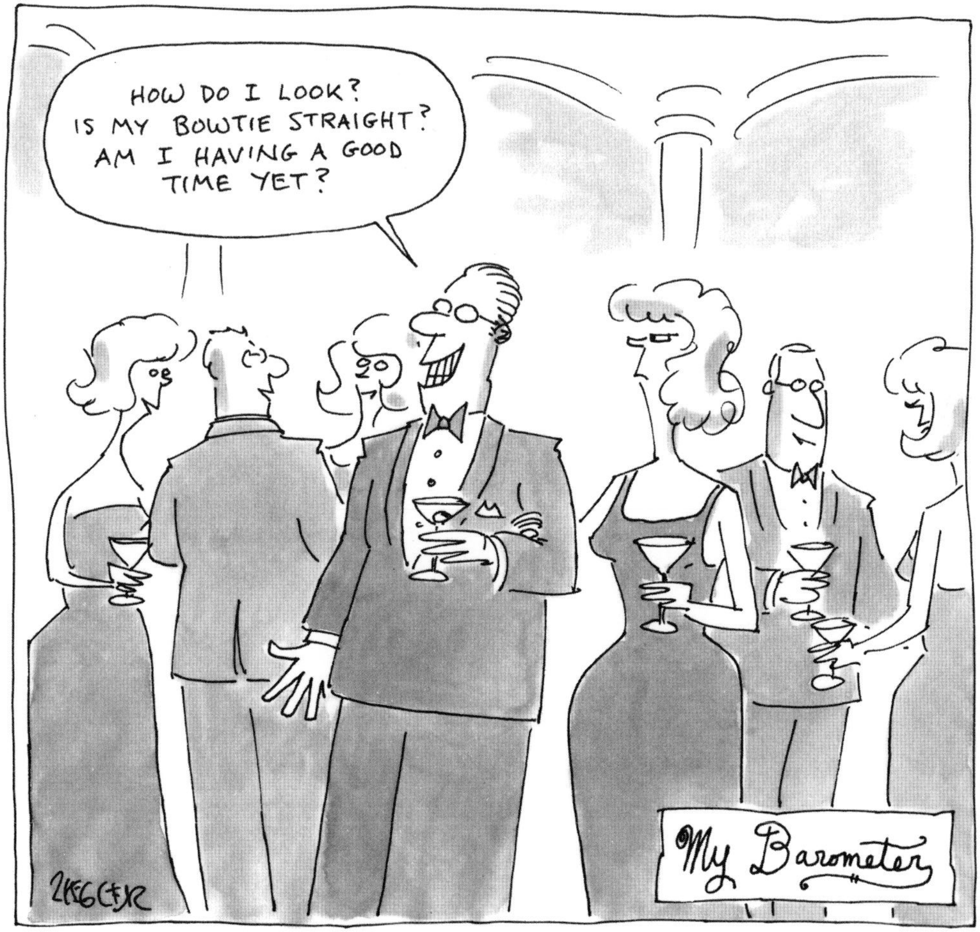
HOW DO I LOOK? IS MY BOWTIE STRAIGHT? AM I HAVING A GOOD TIME YET?
My Barometer

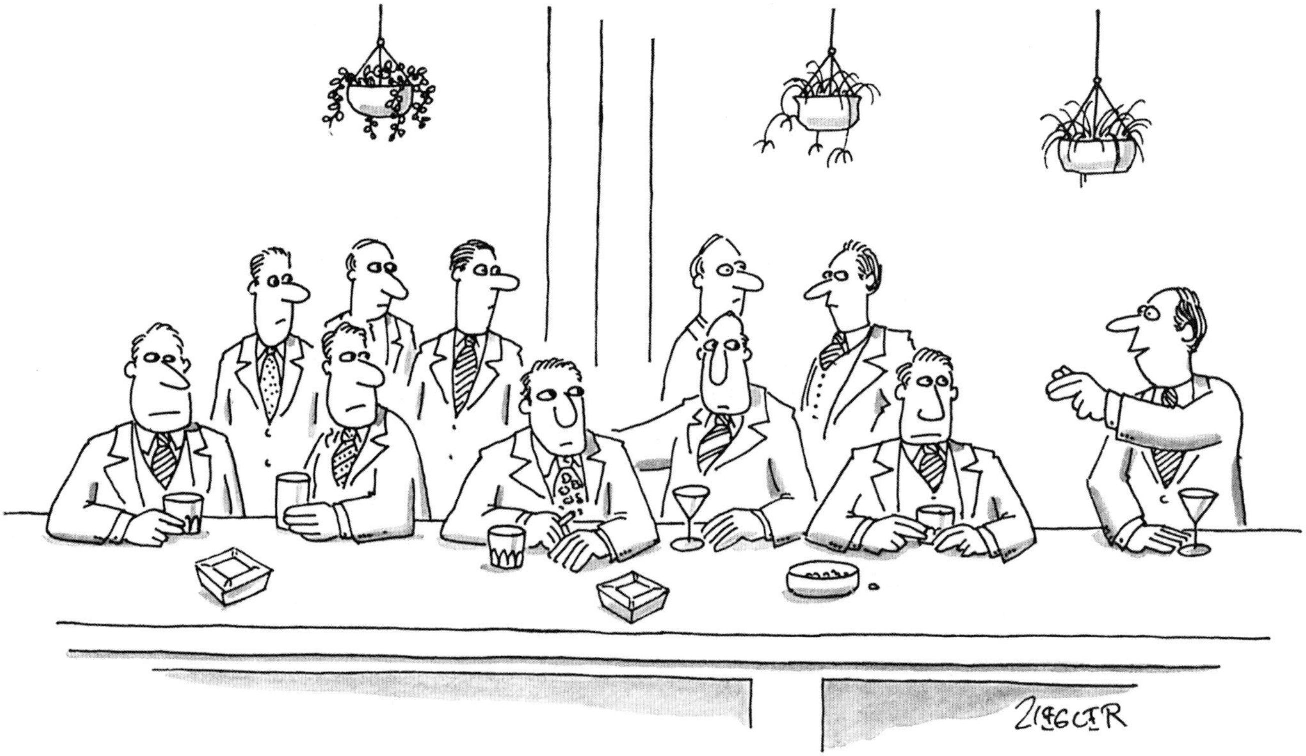
ZIEGLER

"Anyone want my olive?"

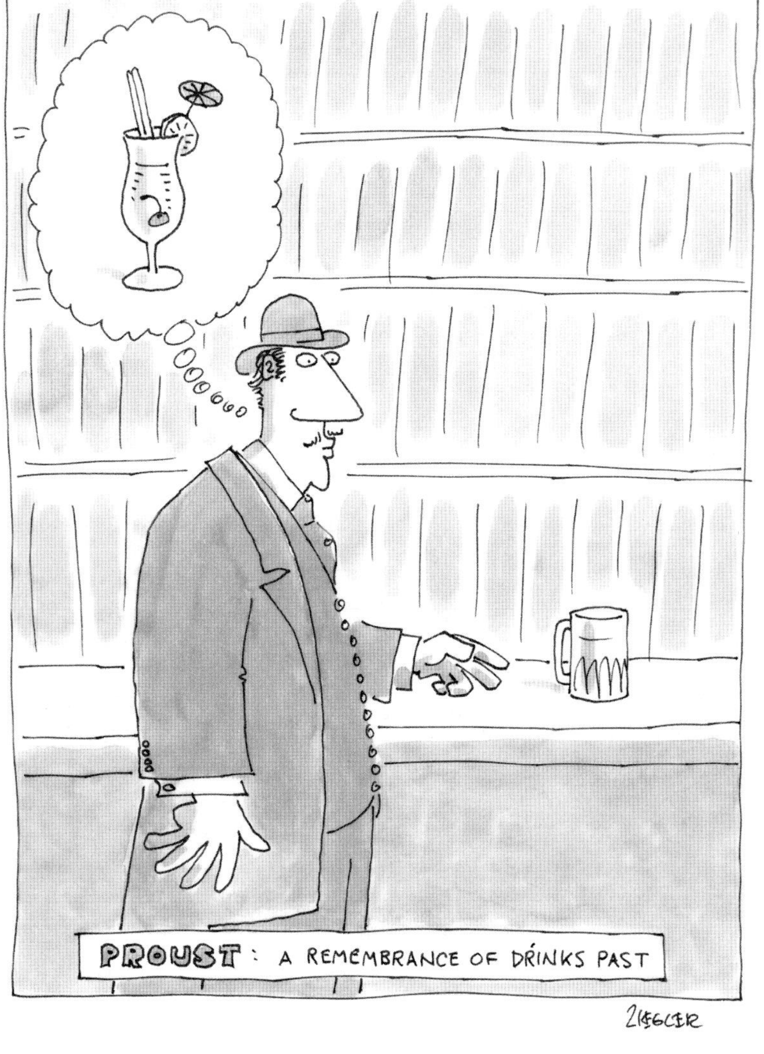
PROUST: A REMEMBRANCE OF DRINKS PAST
ZIEGLER

"Right now we're at a budget impasse. I maintain that you provide an essential service, and my wife feels that you do not."

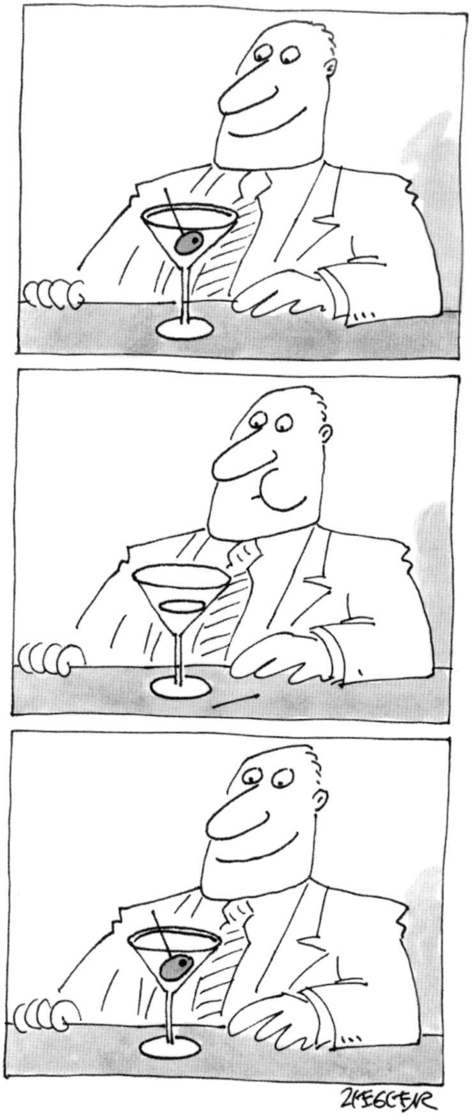
ZIEGLER

"*I'm down here, enjoying a quiet beer at the Stack-o'-Bills-That-I-Can't-Pay Café.*"

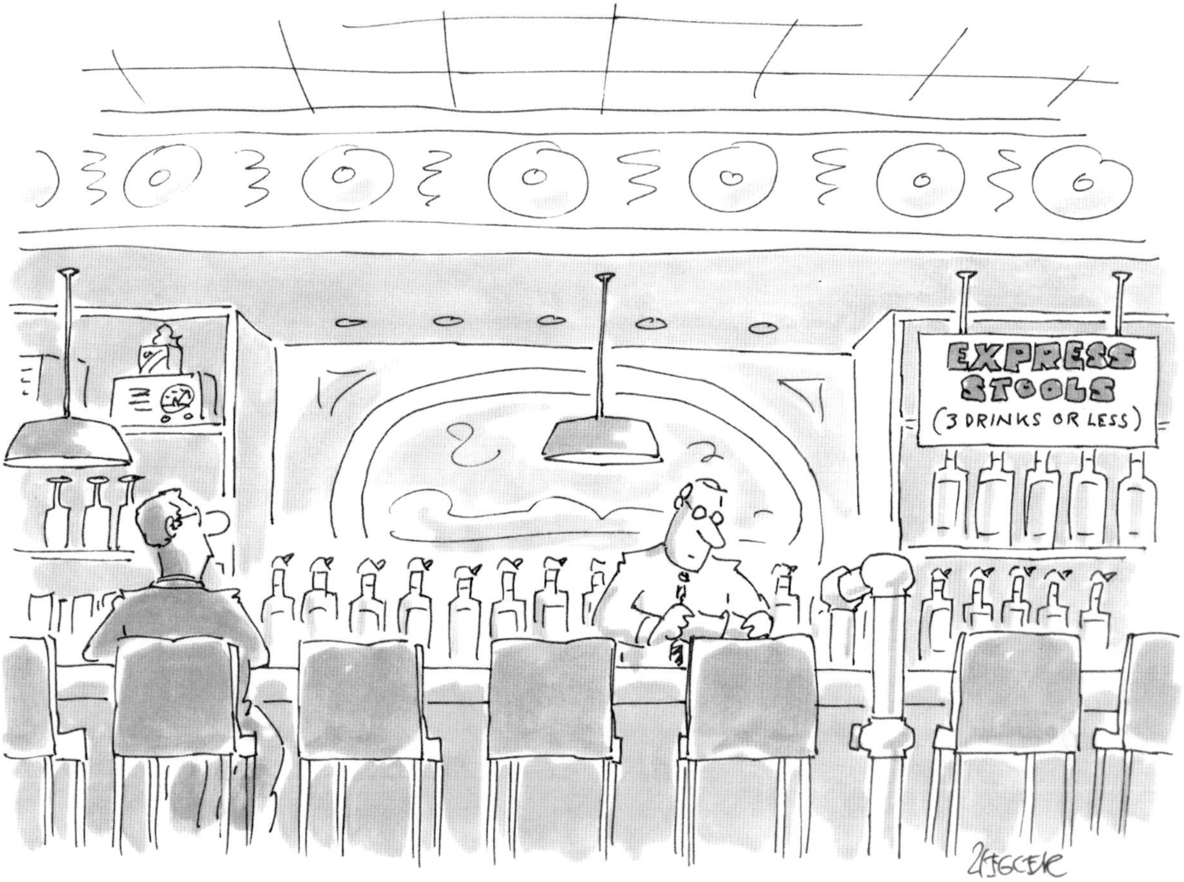
EXPRESS STOOLS
(3 DRINKS OR LESS)

"My wife doesn't understand me, especially when she gets wind of situations like this."

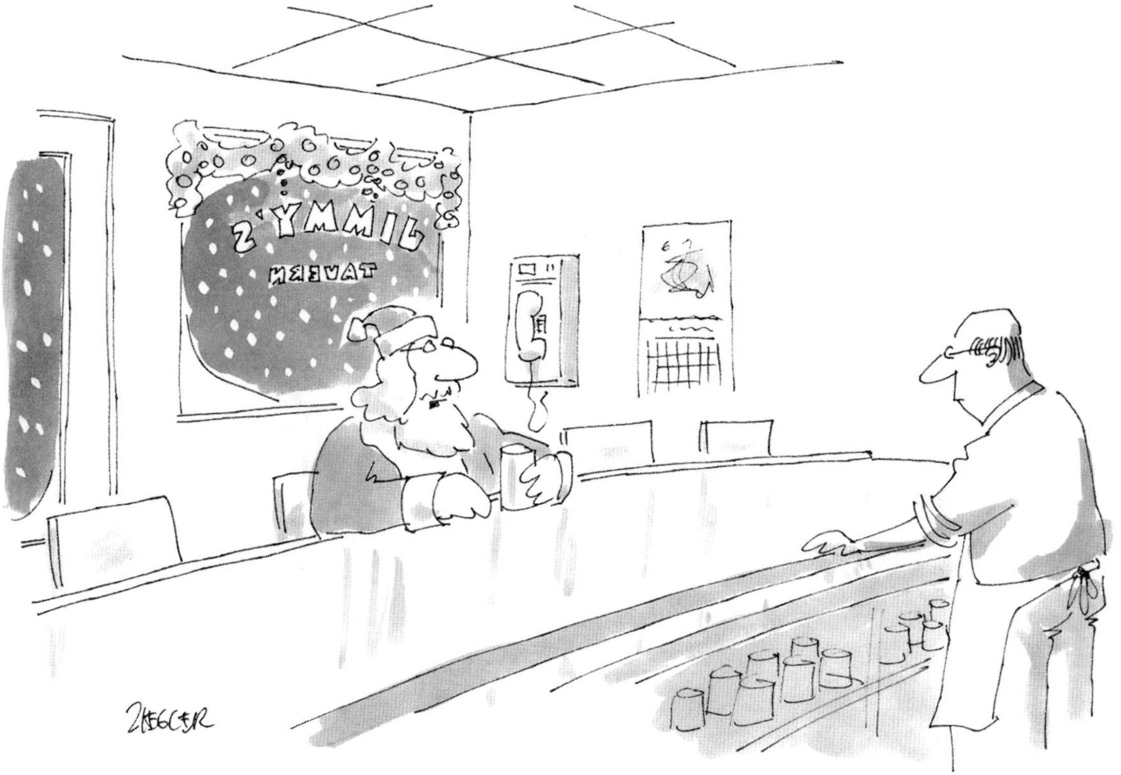
JIMMY'S
TAVERN
ZIEGLER

"How about a six-pack to go, Jimmy, for the elves out in the sled?"

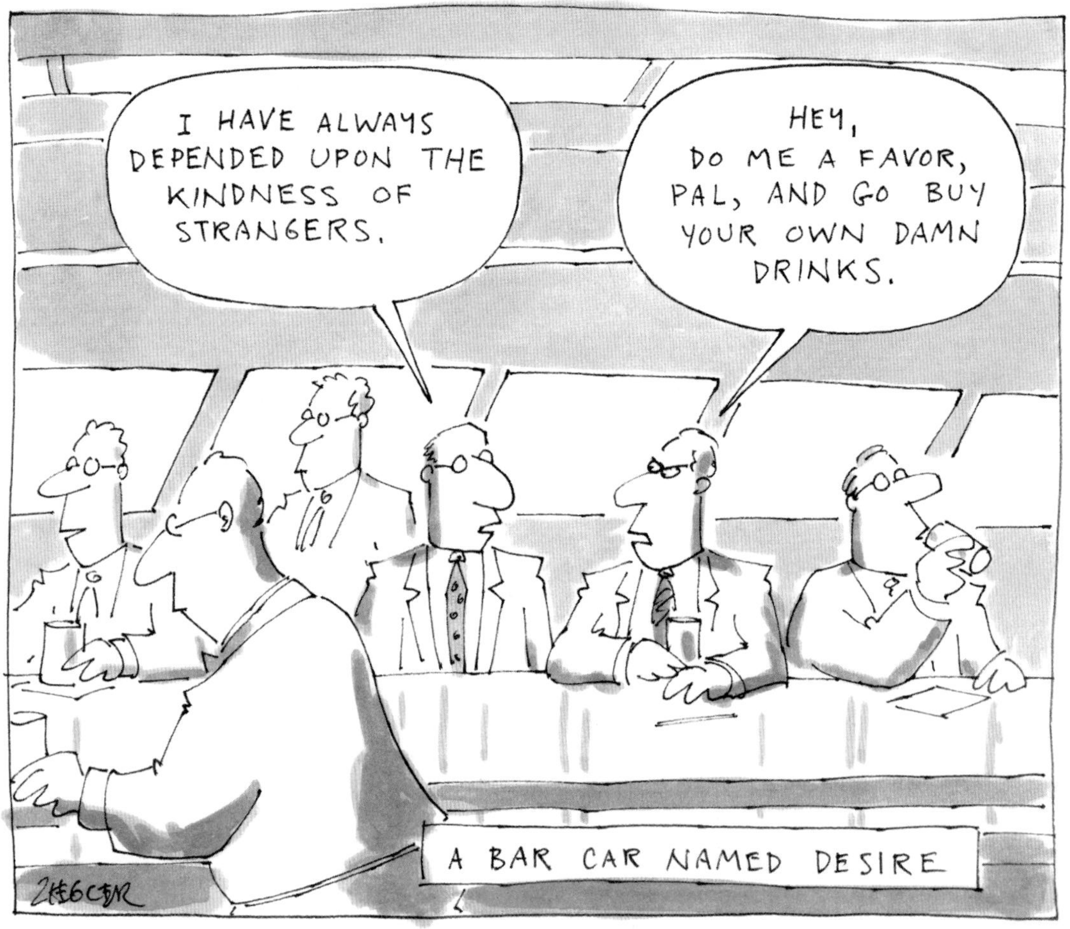
I HAVE ALWAYS DEPENDED UPON THE KINDNESS OF STRANGERS.
HEY, DO ME A FAVOR, PAL, AND GO BUY YOUR OWN DAMN DRINKS.
A BAR CAR NAMED DESIRE
ZIEGLER

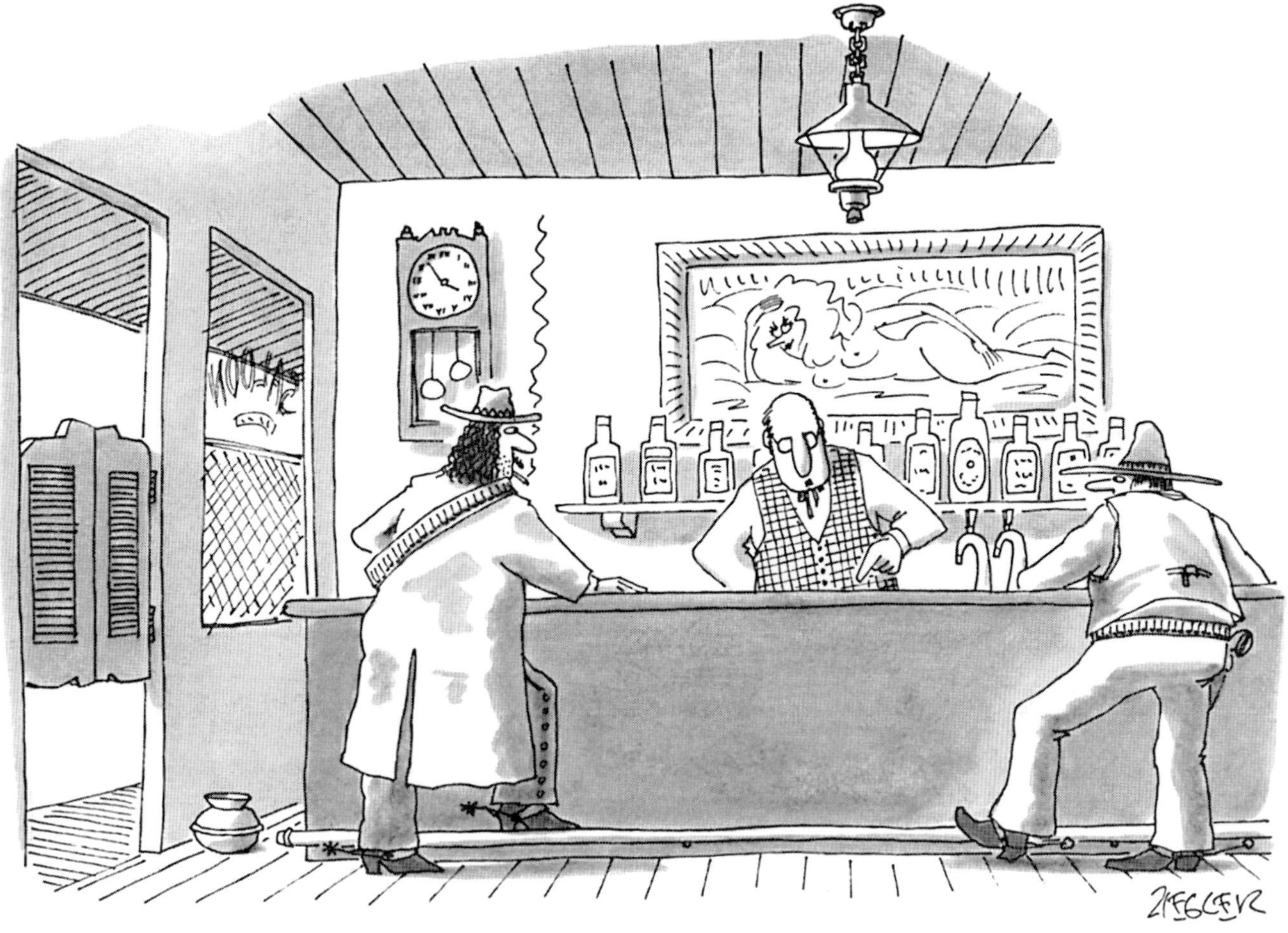

"In bottles we've got Heineken, Kirin, Beck's, and Tsing-Tao. On tap it's Molson and St. Pauli Girl."

"We'd now like to do a song that will barely penetrate your consciousness as you continue to enjoy those faddish cigars and single-malt Scotches."

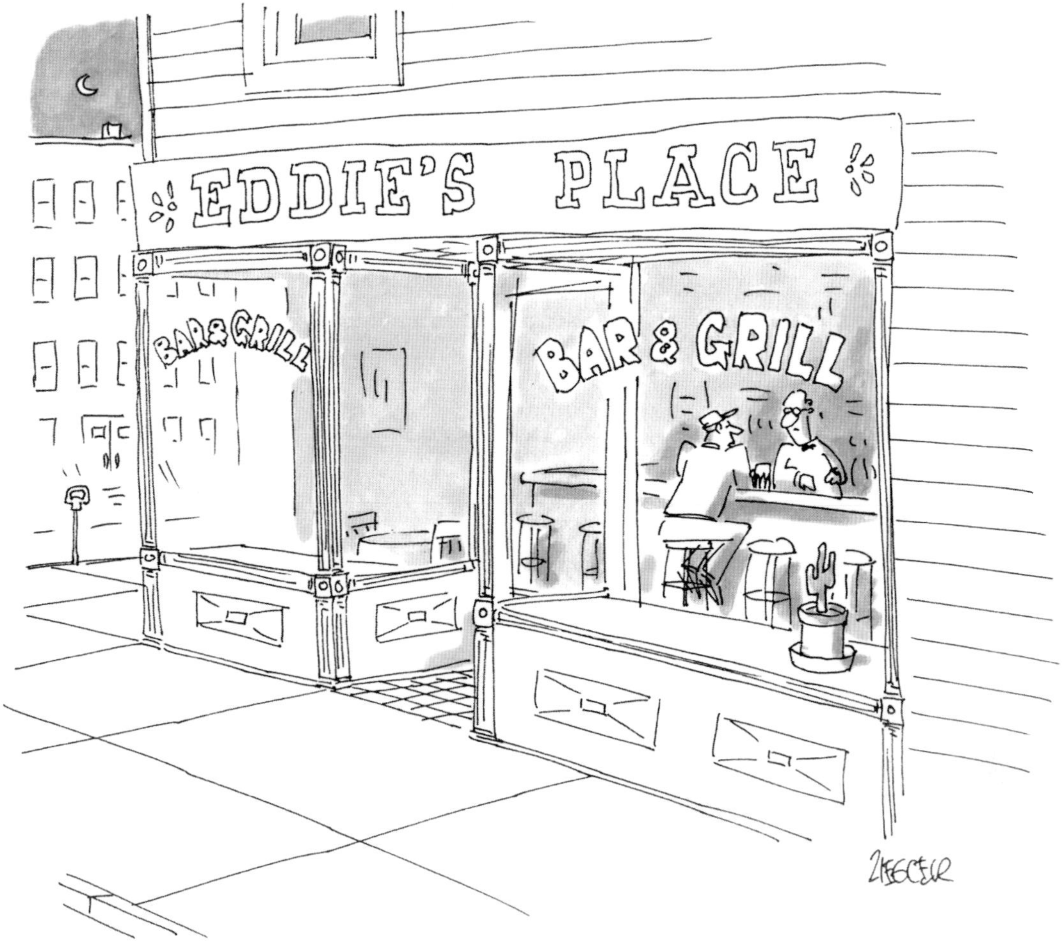
EDDIE'S PLACE
BAR & GRILL
BAR & GRILL
ZIEGLER

"I'm earlier than usual this evening due to an elevated level of chatter at home."

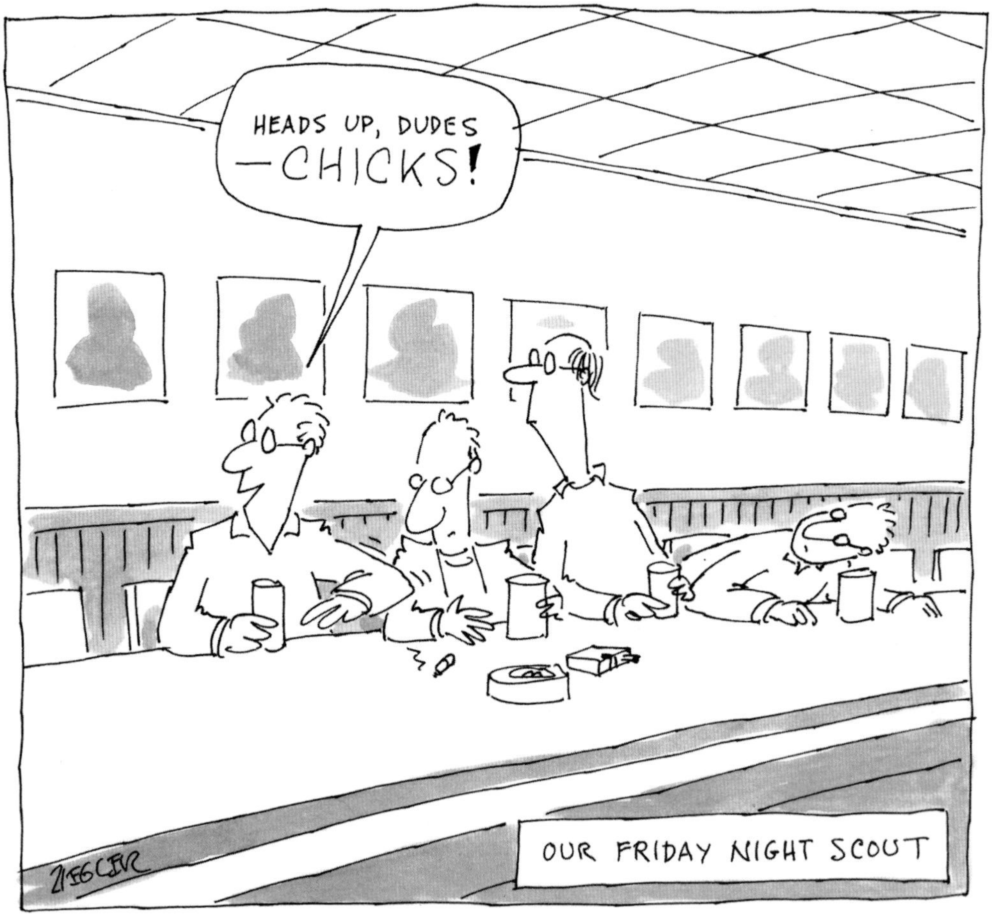
HEADS UP, DUDES —CHICKS!
OUR FRIDAY NIGHT SCOUT
ZIEGLER

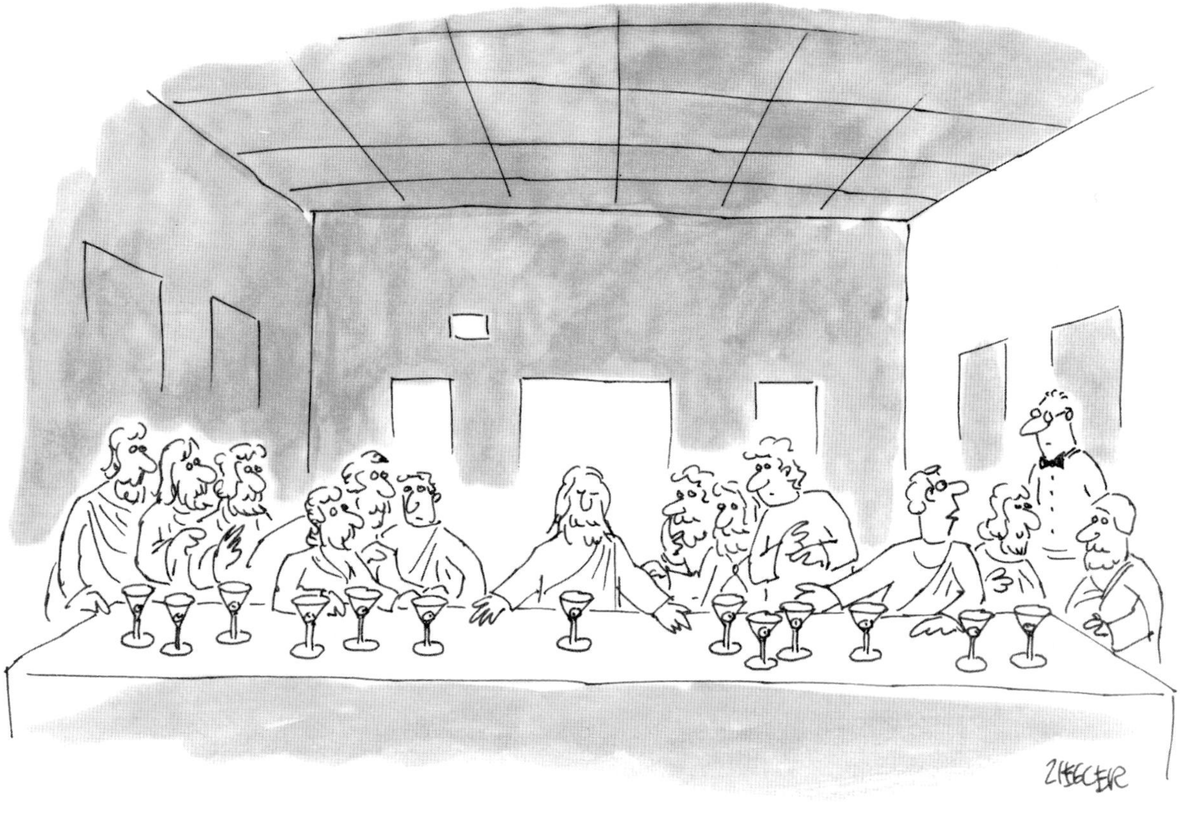
ZIEGLER

"One more round and then we should probably order."

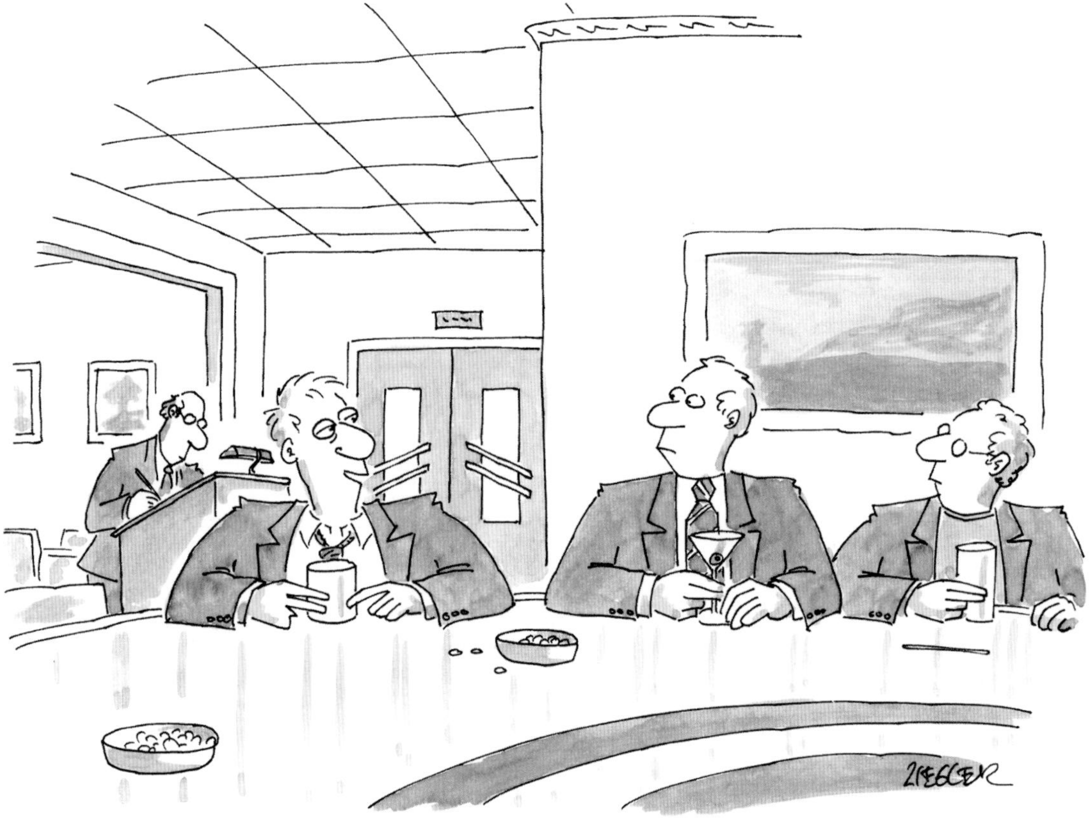
ZIEGLER

"Hey, who wants to hear a great single-malt story?"

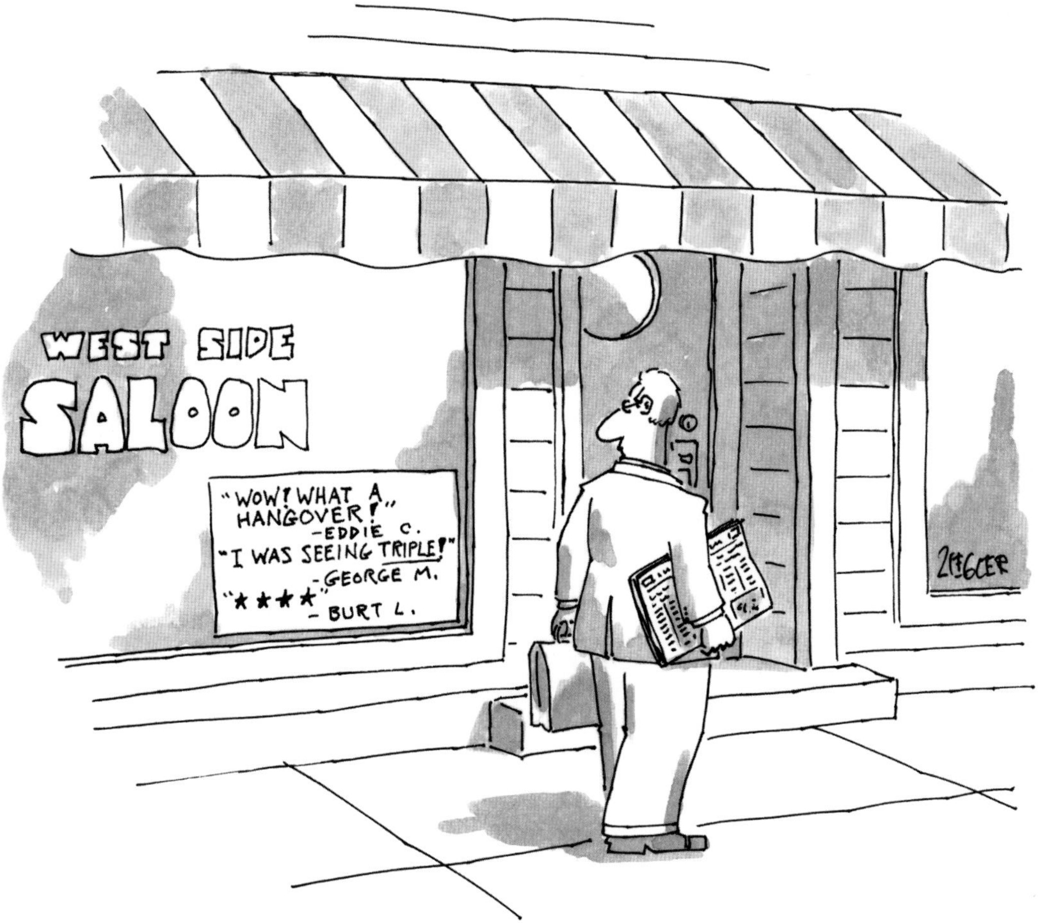
WEST SIDE
SALOON
"WOW! WHAT A HANGOVER!"
-EDDIE C.
"I WAS SEEING TRIPLE!"
-GEORGE M.
"★★★★"
-BURT L.
ZIEGLER

"Oh, we had kids, but we outsourced them years ago."

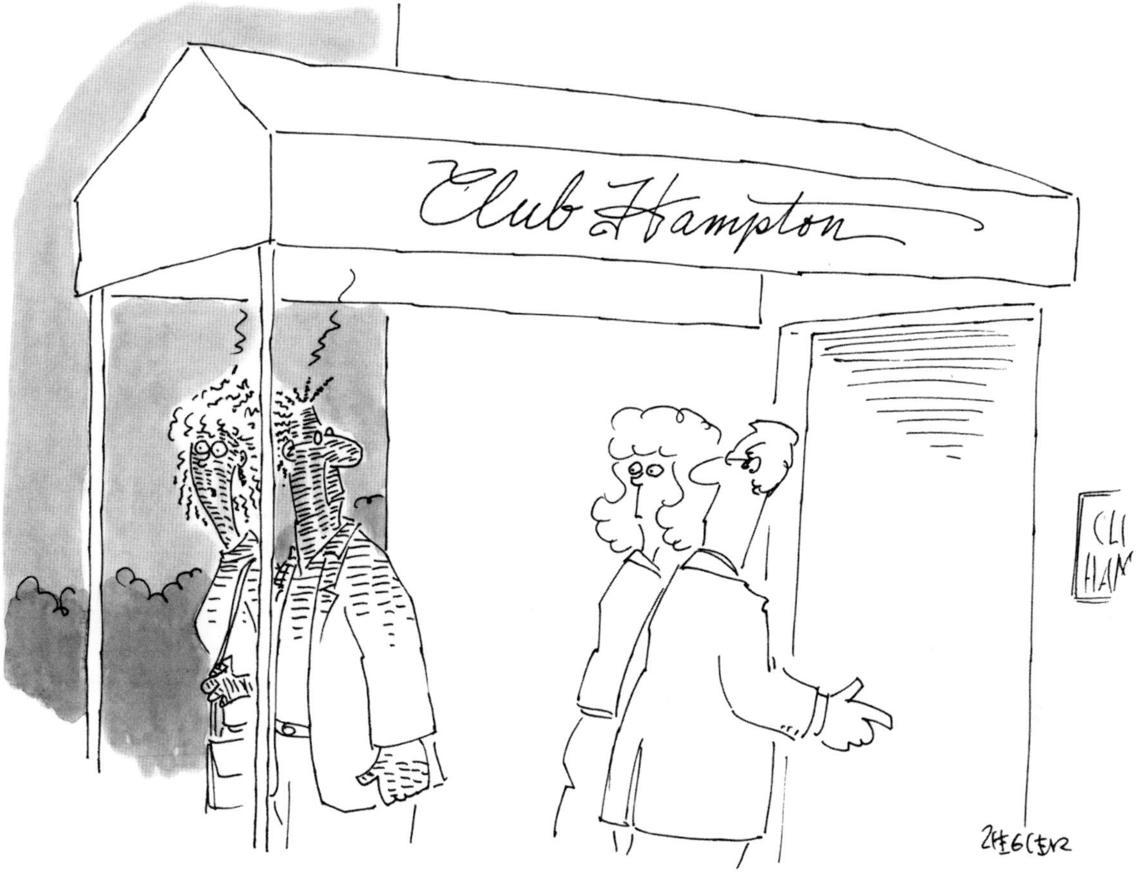
Club Hampton

"Good luck with the secondhand smoke."

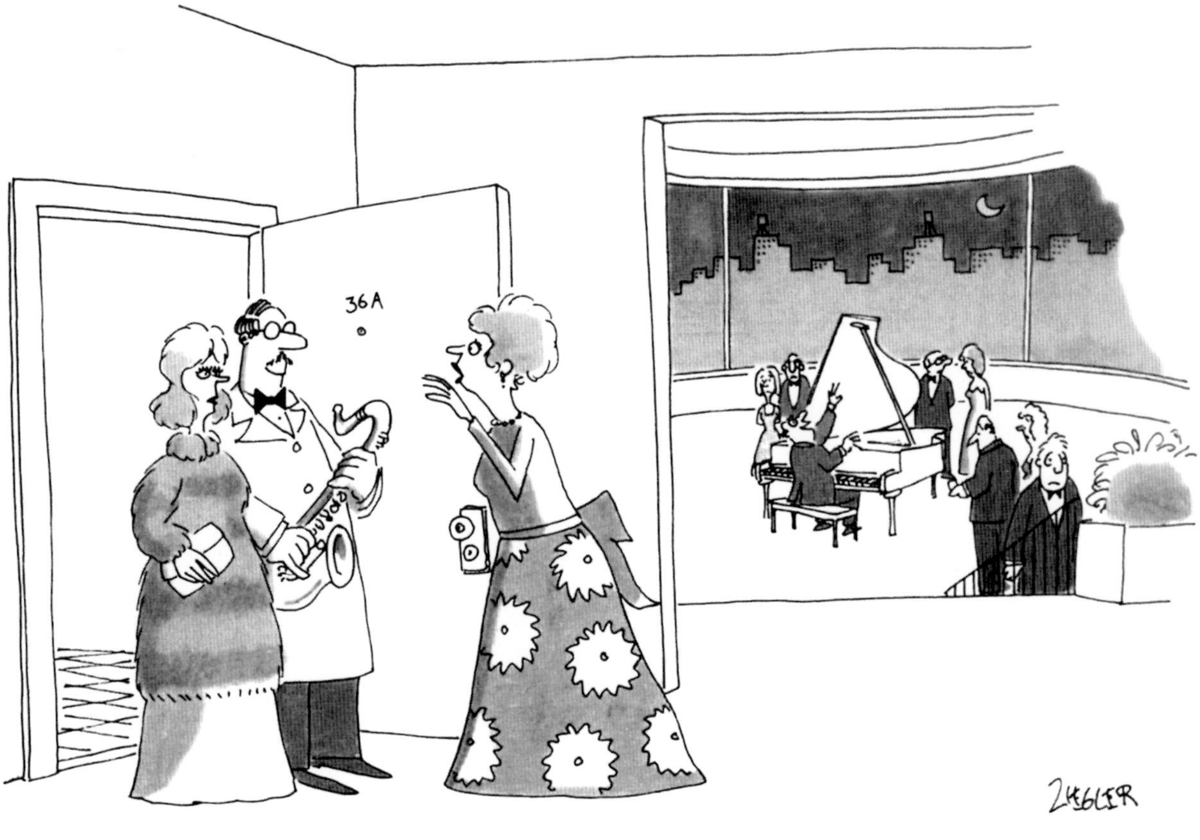
36A
ZIEGLER

"Thank God you're here. Walter has been Barry Manilowing us to death."

"*Have we met? Do we know each other? Can I buy you a drink? Should we date? What about moving in together? Marriage? Children? NO? Not interested? O.K., then*—NEXT!"

"I don't mind the drunk and loud and obnoxious. It's the inevitable Motown medley that makes me cringe."

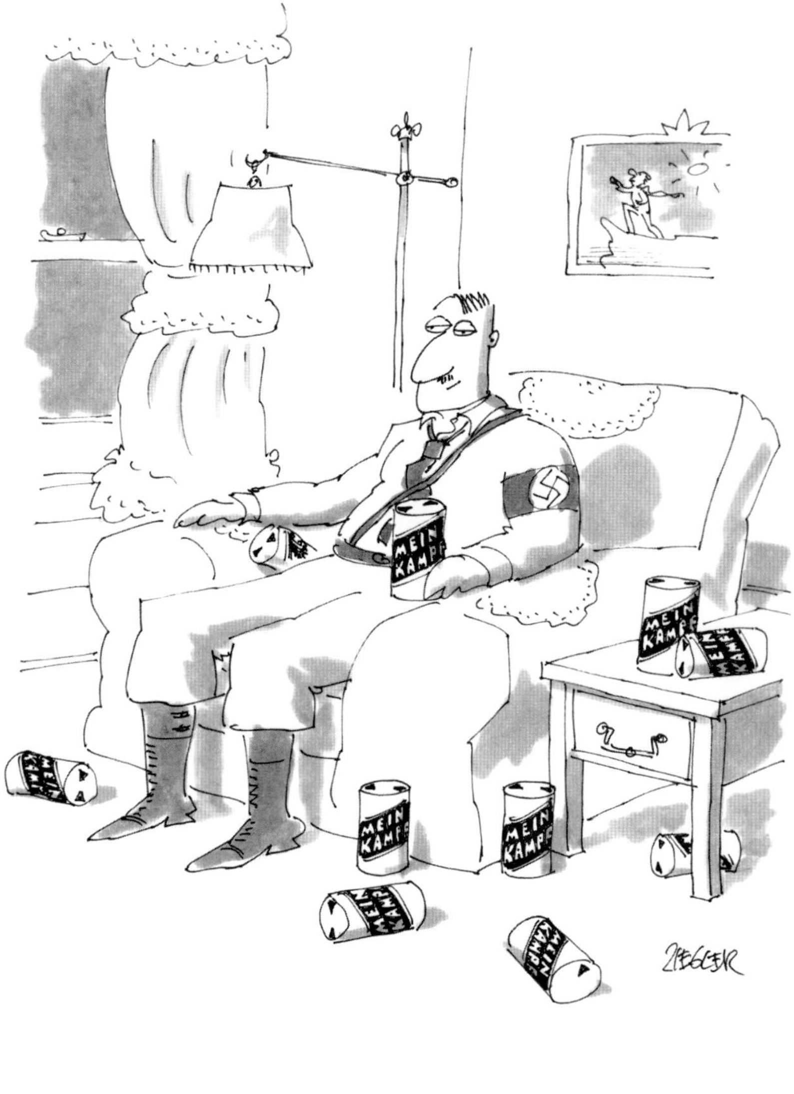
MEIN KAMPF
ZIEGLER

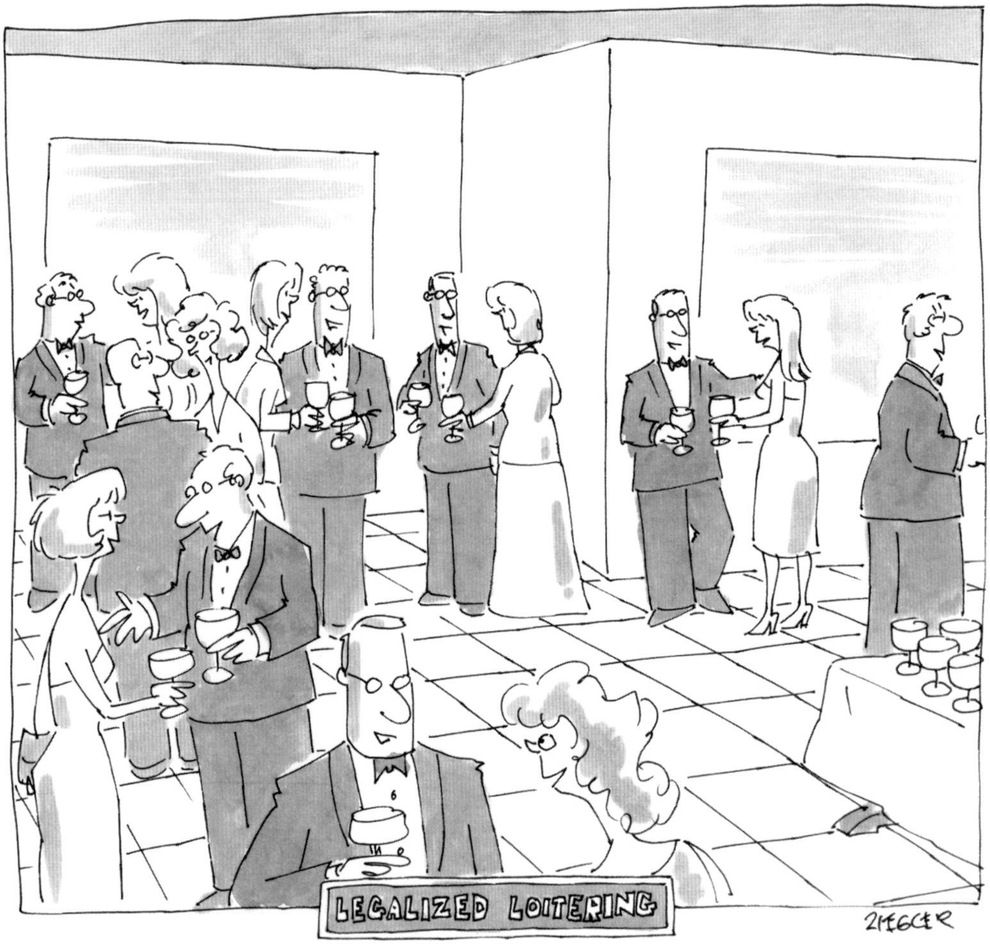
LEGALIZED LOITERING
ZIEGLER

"*Cigarettes used to be a pretty good prop, but they don't seem to work for me anymore.*"

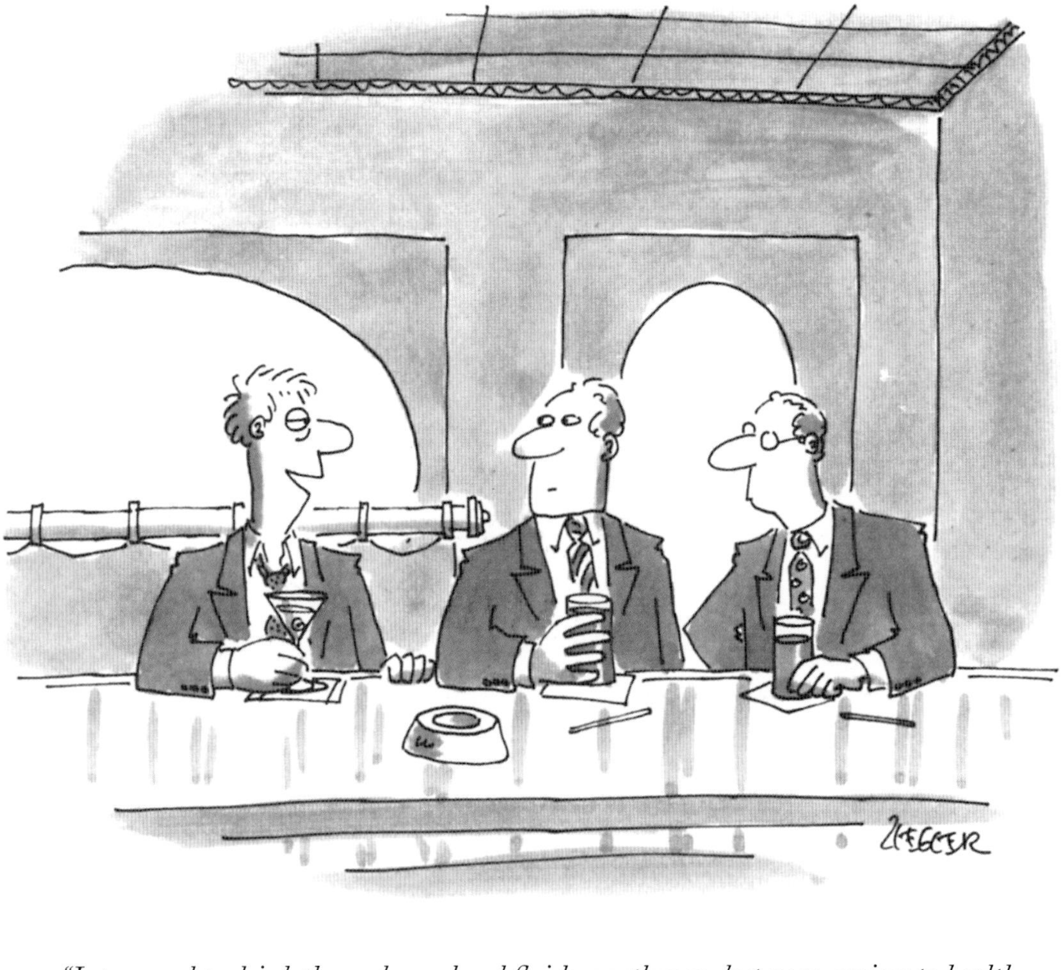
ZIEGLER

"I, too, used to drink the amber-colored fluids, gentlemen, but now, owing to health considerations, I drink only the crystal-clear fluids."

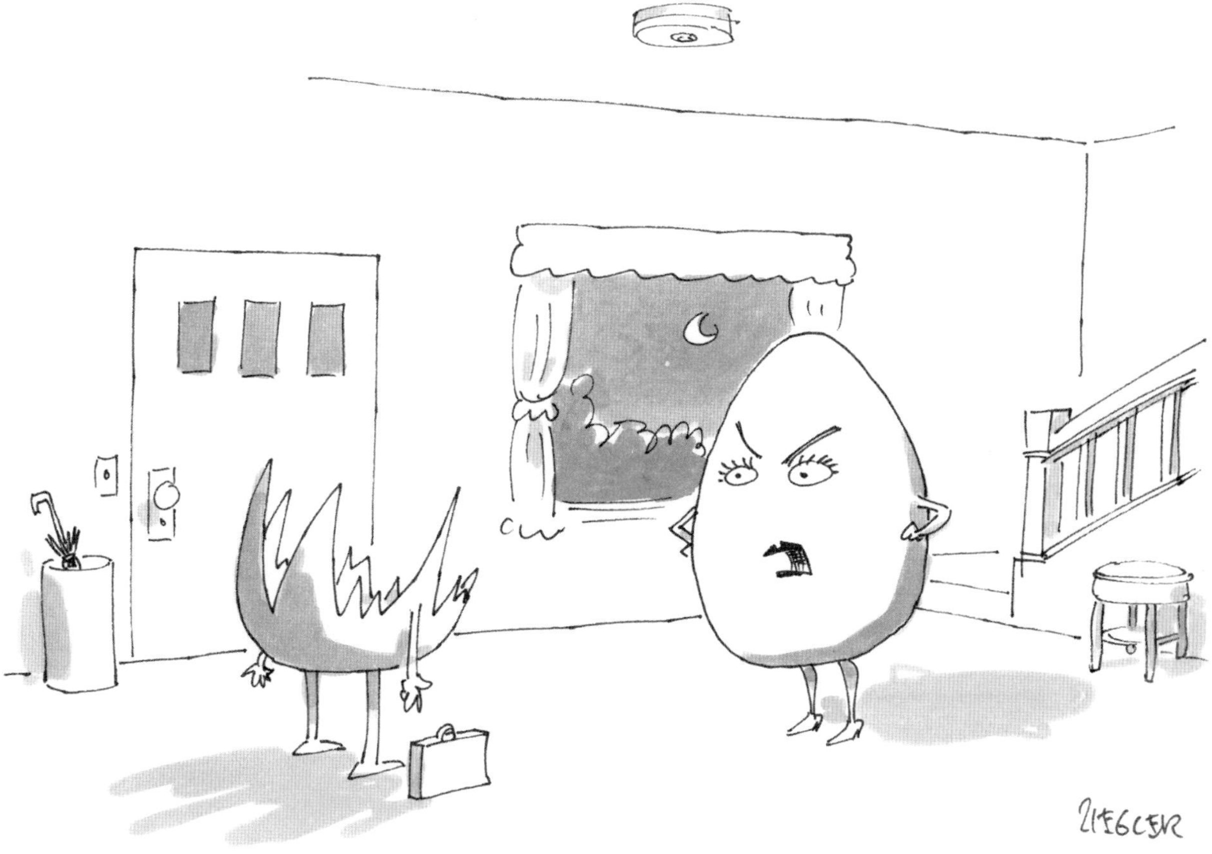
ZIEGLER

"You're late! And don't hand me any of that all the king's horses crap!"

"Here's to the human genome—and its potential in finding, at long last, a cure for the human hangover!"

"When those damn graphic novels started coming out—that's when it all went down the toilet."

"Underneath this placid Brooks Brothers facade, I'm up to my neck in some excellent biker tattoos."

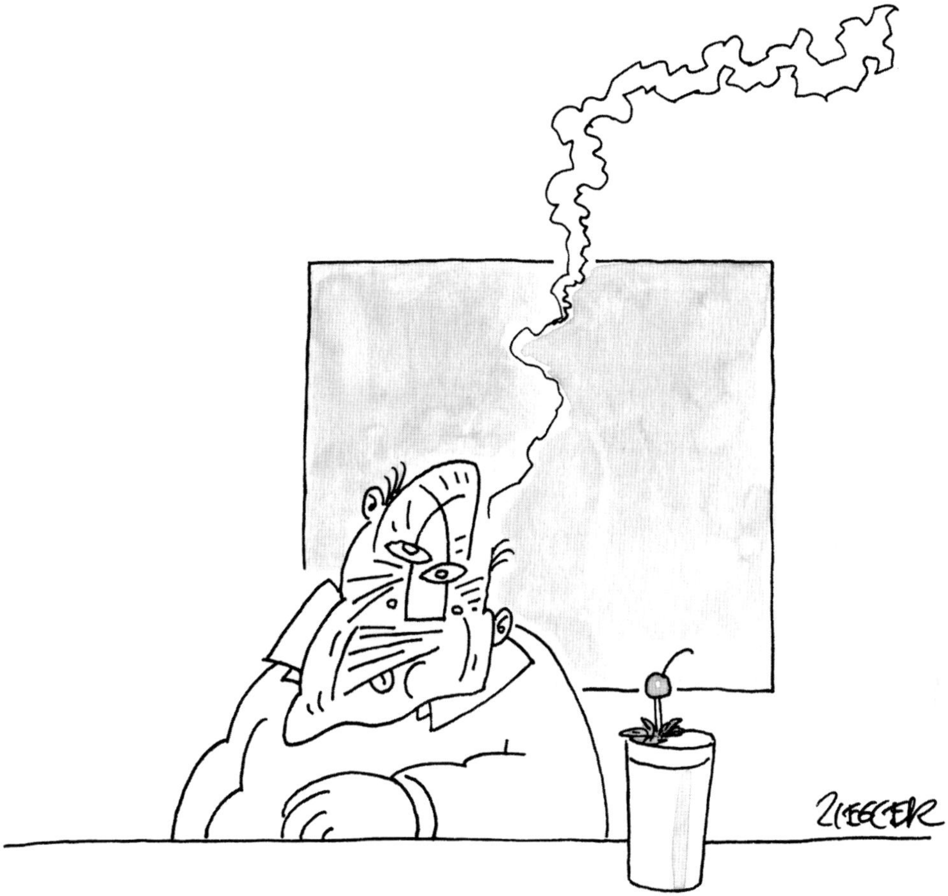
ZIEGLER

"I contemplate Zombie number seventeen"

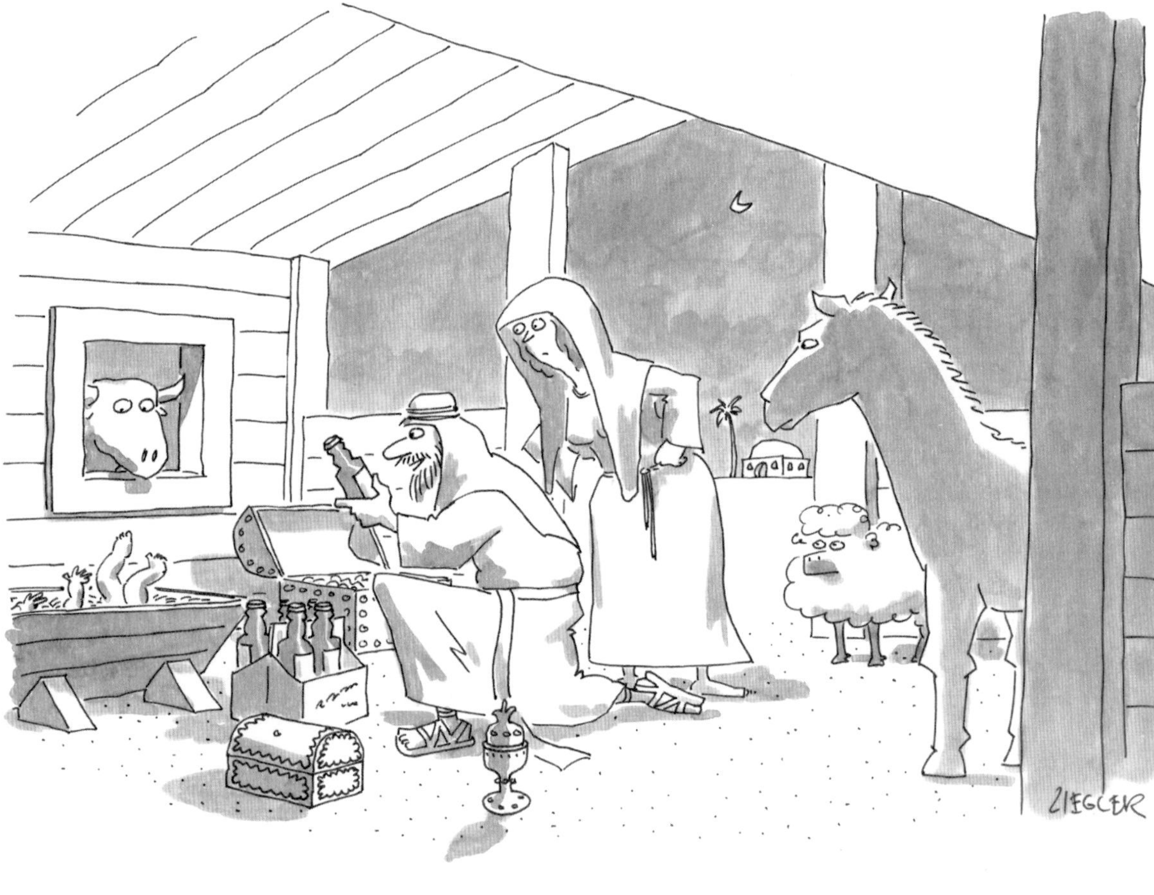
ZIEGLER

"Wow! Gold, frankincense, myrrh—and a six-pack!"

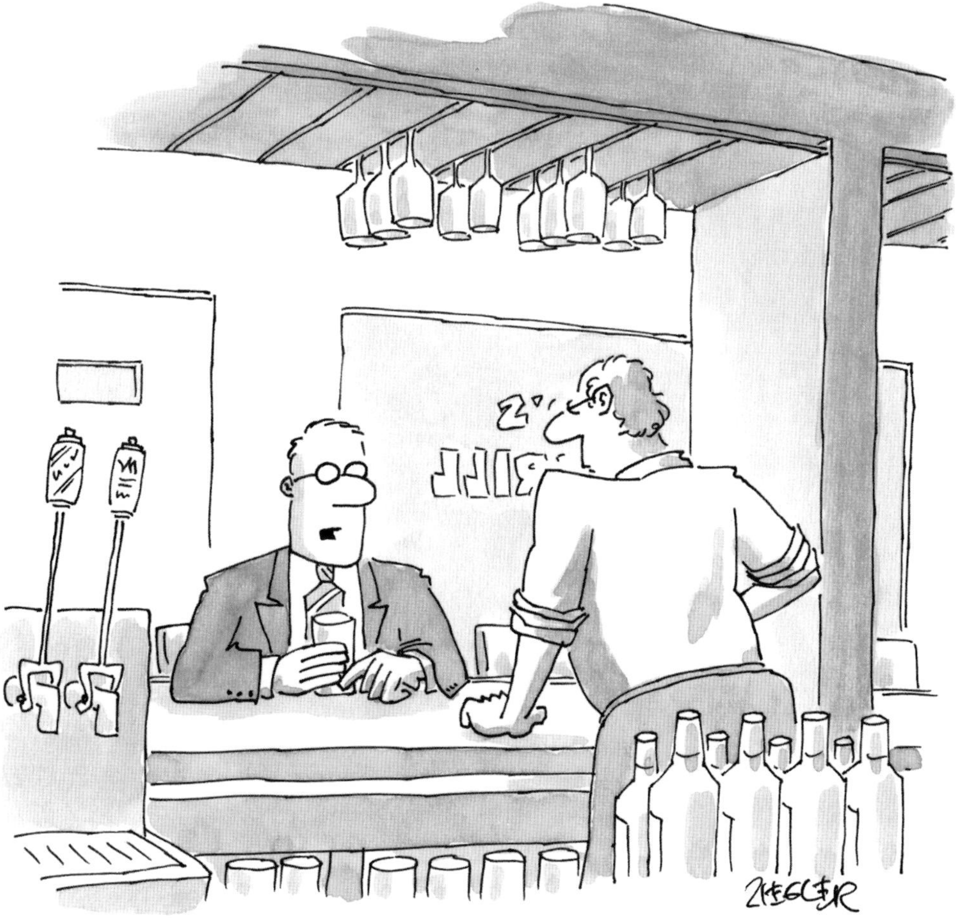
ZIEGLER

"I'm adding an extra hour of booze time here, Al, as a heightened security measure."

"You seem to be having trouble, James, holding up your end of the conversation."

"Honey, I'm home."

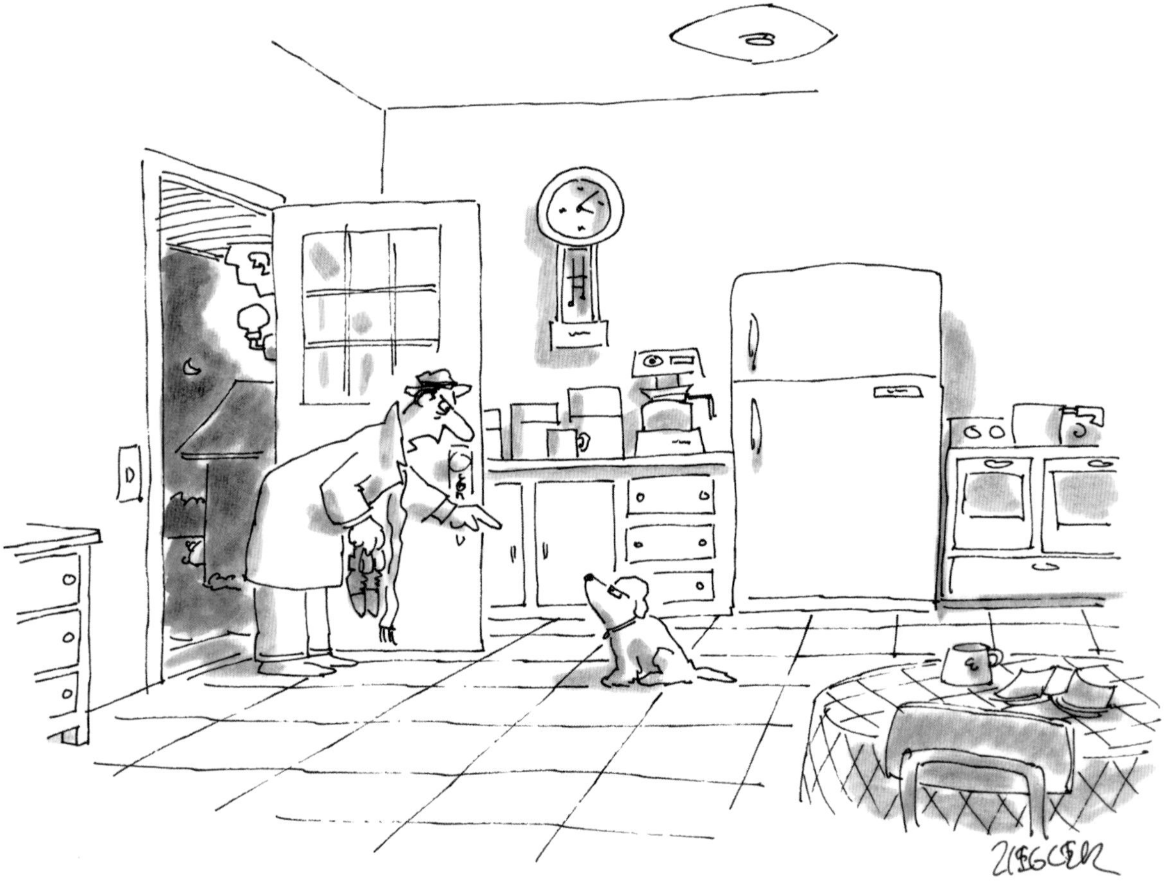
ZIEGLER

"I don't have to explain myself to you!"